The Virgin Mary: A Very Short Introduction

VERY SHORT INTRODUCTIONS are for anyone wanting a stimulating and accessible way into a new subject. They are written by experts, and have been translated into more than 45 different languages.

The series began in 1995, and now covers a wide variety of topics in every discipline. The VSI library currently contains over 650 volumes—a Very Short Introduction to everything from Psychology and Philosophy of Science to American History and Relativity—and continues to grow in every subject area.

Very Short Introductions available now:

For more information visit our website

www.oup.com/vsi/

Mary Joan Winn Leith

THE VIRGIN
MARY

A Very Short Introduction

OXFORD
UNIVERSITY PRESS

Great Clarendon Street, Oxford, OX2 6DP,
United Kingdom

Oxford University Press is a department of the University of Oxford.
It furthers the University's objective of excellence in research, scholarship,
and education by publishing worldwide. Oxford is a registered trade mark of
Oxford University Press in the UK and in certain other countries

First edition published 2021

Impression: 1

Published in the United States of America by Oxford University Press
198 Madison Avenue, New York, NY 10016, United States of America

British Library Cataloguing in Publication Data
Data available

Library of Congress Control Number: 2021939018

ISBN 978-0-19-879491-2

Printed in Great Britain by
Ashford Colour Press Ltd, Gosport, Hampshire

For Rob, Bill, and Tom

Contents

Contents

List of illustrations

Author's note

The author grew up Protestant but, while respectful of religious sensitivities, writes here as a historian, applying the rules of evidence to the topic of the Virgin Mary.

Bible passages are from the *New Revised Standard Translation* unless otherwise indicated.

Chapter 1
Meeting Mary: the surprising virgin

Mary, the mother of Jesus, has a place in the religious consciousness of the 3.8 billion Christians and Muslims who make up more than half the world's population. Muslims and Christians agree on certain basics: that by the power of God a Jewish virgin named Mary ('Mariam' in her native Aramaic language) miraculously became pregnant without sexual intercourse and gave birth to Jesus the prophet, miracle-worker, and Messiah. There are, of course, important differences between the Christian and Muslim Mary, and Christians themselves often differ over the Virgin Mary. Her significance and roles have varied considerably not just today but over the past two millennia of Christianity. A close reading of the New Testament reveals that even Jesus's earliest followers perceived Mary in different ways.

All four of the New Testament Gospels (Matthew, Mark, Luke, John) indicate that Jesus's mother was Jewish, lived in the Galilean village of Nazareth, and apparently bore other children besides Jesus. Three of the Gospels (Matthew, Mark, Luke) record her name: Mary (*Maria* or *Mariam* in Greek, the language of the Gospels). Only Matthew and Luke describe Jesus's miraculous conception by Mary. Only John places Mary at the Crucifixion of her son. The other three Gospels omit Jesus's mother from their list of women at the Crucifixion. In no Gospel is Mary a witness to Jesus's resurrection. If we turn to the very earliest writings about

Jesus in the Bible, the letters of the apostle Paul, we read simply that Jesus was 'born of a woman' (Galatians 4:4) with no hint of a miraculous conception, whereas Paul refers numerous times to Jesus's brothers. If Christian scriptures give varying accounts of Mary, we should hardly be surprised that in the course of 2,000 years, perceptions have evolved, and in various directions.

The Virgin Mary may be one of the most famous women in history, but she has also been subject to misunderstandings, unquestioned presuppositions, and misinformation, even among her devotees. A 2013 survey of Americans by the Pew Research Center showed that 73 per cent of Americans believe Jesus was born of a virgin, but anecdotal evidence suggests that most Americans erroneously assume the term 'Immaculate Conception' refers to Mary's virginal conception of Jesus. In fact, the Immaculate Conception is a theological doctrine professed exclusively by Roman Catholics to refer to the moment Mary was conceived in her mother's womb.

Furthermore, even in the 21st century when few would disagree that the Jewish Virgin Mary from Roman-ruled Palestine would have had Mediterranean features, the prevailing stereotype about Mary's appearance is still blonde, as well as humble and submissive. The majority Protestant and Catholic population of western Europe and the USA also tends to forget the millions of Orthodox Christians on whose icons Mary's hair is hidden under a veil, her eyes dark, her complexion olive, golden, or even black. As for the submissive Mary, since the late 20th century, Catholic liberation theologians have countered that Mary is an eloquent advocate for social justice, a mother resisting an oppressive state. They hear revolution in the words of newly pregnant Mary's song, the *Magnificat* (Luke 1:46–55),

> [the Lord] has shown strength with his arm; he has scattered the
> proud in the thoughts of their hearts. He has brought down the

powerful from their thrones and lifted up the lowly; he has filled the hungry with good things and sent the rich away empty.

It may also come as a surprise that the Virgin Mary has been, and continues to be, a religiously divisive figure. For example, given her indisputable Jewishness, it is a tragic irony that the enormously popular medieval stories about Mary's miracles are riddled with anti-Judaism. In the 16th century, as the Protestant Reformation spread across Europe, the Virgin became a flashpoint for intra-Christian polemics. To Protestants, Catholic veneration of the Virgin looked like idolatry and a perversion of the Bible's portrayal of Mary as a normal human. Despite reformer Martin Luther's lifelong Marian devotion, Mary essentially disappeared from Protestant theology, in part because among Protestants, the Virgin came to symbolize all that they were 'protesting' about Catholicism.

Still, notwithstanding pervasive American anti-Catholicism, 19th-century Protestants like Harriet Beecher Stowe, author of *Uncle Tom's Cabin*, could write approvingly of Mary as an exemplar of femininity, maternity, and domesticity. Recent decades have seen tentative steps to bring Mary back into the Protestant fold. As for Catholics, at the mid-16th-century Council of Trent the Catholic Church reaffirmed its devotion to the Virgin, largely dismissing the Reformers' objections. Catholic allegiance to the Virgin rose to unprecedented heights of ardour with the promotion of new pilgrimage sites like Lourdes in France and with the triumphant papal proclamations of Mary's Immaculate Conception in 1854 and Assumption into heaven in 1950.

For a glimpse into the kaleidoscopic variety of Marian traditions, let us consider two images. I could have chosen famous artworks like Michelangelo's *Pietà* or Raphael's *Sistine Madonna*, but two less renowned and highly contrasting sculptures will provide an

1. *Mary of the Miraculous Medal* (1830).

entry into many of the big issues about Mary that this book will
discuss. The first, *Mary of the Miraculous Medal*, originated in
1830 France (Figure 1). The second is 2005's *The Virgin Mother* by
British artist Damien Hirst (Figure 2).

Both are metal sculptures, but otherwise they seem to come from
different planets, and not just because one is a miniature relief
and the other a free-standing figure 33 feet (10 metres) high.
Nevertheless, together they reveal an array of long-standing and
traditional beliefs regarding the Virgin Mary.

2. *The Virgin Mother*, Damien Hirst (2005), bronze, h. 33 ft (installed at Lever House, New York, 2005).

Mary of the Miraculous Medal can be considered the prototype of the submissive stereotype. The composition was inspired by the earliest of many high-profile modern apparitions of the Virgin that included Lourdes (1858), Fátima in Portugal (1917), and Medjugorje in Bosnia-Herzegovina (1981 to present). In 1830, Catholic visionary Catherine Labouré reported that the Virgin had dictated to her every detail of a new medal including the motto, 'Mary, conceived without sin, pray for us who turn to you.' The phrase 'conceived without sin' proclaims Mary's Immaculate Conception, a doctrine centred on the belief that from the moment of her conception, Mary was freed from all sin including the original sin Christians believe humans inherited from Adam and Eve.

Since the Council of Trent, this abstract doctrine had been visualized in the Roman Catholic world just as we see on the medal, by the solitary figure of Mary in the heavens (see Figure 16, Chapter 7). Mary's downcast eyes, in fact, signalled not only humility but purity, especially sexual purity. Early Christian writers linked the power of sight with sexual desire and advised devout virgins, both male and female, to preserve their virtue by averting their eyes from temptation. Immaculate Conception iconography also surrounded Mary with the rays of light featured on the medal, an allusion to the woman 'clothed in the sun with the moon at her feet and crowned with twelve stars' described in the Book of Revelation (12:1). Intended by the 1st-century author of Revelation as a personification of Israel, this visionary woman framed in celestial light came to symbolize the Church and later was associated with the Virgin Mary's Assumption and coronation as queen of heaven. The medal thus glorifies Mary in her role as exalted and transcendent queen.

At the same time, the second half of the medal's motto, 'pray for us who turn to you', links Mary the lofty sovereign with her human subjects. The motto is symbolized most palpably by Mary's cloak and her open hands. In the medieval tradition of the *Mater*

Misericordiae, the 'Mother of Mercies' shelters her suppliants in the folds of her cloak and intercedes with Christ in heaven on their behalf. Tradition dictates that Mary's motherhood gives her unique persuasive power with Jesus. Much earlier, in the Byzantine era, Mary's cloak itself possessed special protective powers as one of the first Marian miracle-working relics.

Finally, Mary stands barefoot on a globe encircled by a snake. The snake symbolizes Satan, whose power over the world is crushed underfoot by Mary as the New Eve untarnished by original sin. Starting with the New Testament writings of Paul, the Adam and Eve story signified disaster for all humans that could only be repaired by Jesus's atoning death on the cross. For Paul, Jesus was the New Adam and within a century Mary was identified as the corresponding New Eve. The 2nd-century Church Father Justin Martyr maintained that the virgin Eve's deadly blunder in succumbing to Satan in the Garden of Eden had been reversed when the Virgin Mary said 'yes' to the Angel Gabriel: 'Here am I, the servant of the Lord; let it be with me according to your word' (Luke 1:38). Thus, *Mary of the Miraculous Medal* presents a paradoxical tension between Mary as humble young girl, remote queen of heaven, and vigilant advocate for those who call upon her. Yet there is one aspect of Mary's identity, one might even call it her signature role, that the medal acknowledges only indirectly: her motherhood.

Mary's motherhood is front and centre in Damien Hirst's *The Virgin Mother*. No less than the *Miraculous Medal*, *The Virgin Mother* reflects a broad range of Marian traditions and theological doctrines, all of them based on Mary's motherhood. Indeed, every visually disturbing aspect of the figure—the nude and pregnant body whose womb shelters an embryo, the physicality expressed in outsized scale, the flayed skin peeled back to reveal sinews, bone, and arteries, even the erect nipples that echo the upward tilt of the Virgin's glance—all these elements derive from traditional, long-held Christian beliefs about the mother of Jesus. In a real

7

sense, what Hirst has created with *The Virgin Mother* is a complex sermon about Mary that challenges believers to confront the implications of essential Christian beliefs.

The most shocking attribute of *The Virgin Mother* is probably her nudity. The sexual connotations of the nude female figure here fly in the face of traditional ideas about Mary's purity; after all, tradition dictates that Mary's body be covered from head to foot. Furthermore, given taboos around displaying nude pregnant bodies, the fact that this nude is also pregnant makes the figure all the more disturbing. Yet the *The Virgin Mother*'s pregnant nudity pronounces Mary's freedom from original sin, the principle at the core of the *Miraculous Medal*. *The Virgin Mother*, like the *Miraculous Medal*, proclaims Mary as the New Eve. In Christian tradition, after Adam and Eve's disobedience, nudity became the embodied symbol of humanity's shame, sin, and inclination toward Satan. If Mary is the New Eve, who by giving birth to Jesus participates in the restoration of human perfection, then the naked *The Virgin Mother* reminds Christian viewers that before the onset of sin, before the disobedience in the Garden, nudity symbolized the perfection of God's human creatures. *The Virgin Mother*'s nudity expresses the perfect intimacy that Adam and Eve enjoyed with God in Eden. After all, in their face-to-face encounters with God they were completely naked. As the foetus enclosed in *The Virgin Mother*'s willing womb, Jesus promises restored intimacy between God and humans.

Despite its scale and its unconventional composition, *The Virgin Mother* emerges from the same devotional tradition that inspired so many images of the Madonna and Child. Wonderingly, *The Virgin Mother* rests a protective hand over her swollen belly with the same gesture made by visibly pregnant Renaissance *del parto* ('about to give birth') Virgins, most famously Piero della Francesca's *Madonna del Parto* of 1467 (see Figure 13, Chapter 6). Hirst's seemingly transgressive portrayal of Jesus as a foetus in the womb rather than a baby in his mother's arms is the artist's way of shaking the viewer out of complacence. Even here, however, *The Virgin Mother* has precedents. In Byzantine renderings of the *Panagia Platytera* (Greek, 'All Holy One, More Spacious [than the Heavens]'), a tiny figure of the infant Jesus looks out from his mother's womb. And from at least the 12th century, artists gave Mary a transparent womb in two familiar scenes: the Annunciation, when Gabriel announces the news of Jesus to Mary (see Figure 10b, Chapter 5) and the Visitation, when Mary visits her cousin Elizabeth to celebrate their miraculous pregnancies. *The Virgin Mother* demands that viewers confront the theological magnitude of Mary's motherhood which was the basis of her earliest official Christian title, *Theotokos*, Greek for 'The One Who Gives Birth to God'.

The 4th-century poet Ephraim of Syria, addressing Jesus in his 'Nativity Hymn 11', exclaims in wonder, 'The womb of your mother overthrew the order of all!' The sculpture's unmistakably human baby points to a cornerstone of Christian belief, that Jesus was God incarnate, a term that comes from the Latin word for flesh, *carnis*, and means 'en-fleshed'. In other words, Jesus had to become incarnated as human in order to deliver humans from sin. Thus, besides sinlessness and the promise of reconciliation between God and humans, *The Virgin Mother*'s nudity and her foetus accentuate the humanity of Mary and Jesus. Jesus's divinity comes from God the Father, but Jesus's humanity came from his human mother, Mary, a fact inescapably emphasized by *The Virgin Mother*'s hyper-real flayed skin. While on a superficial level this is the artist's homage to the popular 'Visible Man' and 'Visible Woman' anatomical models of the 1960s, the statue's lifelike flesh and blood foreshadow the price that—each in their own way— Jesus and his mother are fated to pay. In the words of St Catherine of Siena writing in the 14th century about Mary and Jesus at the Crucifixion,

> Oh, sweetest love, this was the sword that struck your mother's
> heart and soul. The Son was physically pierced, and so was his

mother, since his flesh was hers. This was only right, since that flesh was her own: he had taken his flesh from her.

From the 1st century to the 21st century, Christians have often ignored or forgotten the Christian belief that unless Jesus was fully human with all its limitations, his death could not bring about human salvation. This comes through in the earliest known reference to Jesus's mother outside the Gospels. In the early 2nd century, Ignatius of Antioch attacked certain Christian groups who denied that Jesus could have been human. This first Christian heresy was called 'Docetism' from the Greek, 'to seem'. Docetists believed Jesus only 'seemed' human because, they argued, if Jesus were truly human with all the physical indignities that go with a human body then he could not have been truly divine. To the contrary, Ignatius insisted on the ultimately winning position that Jesus was divine *and* human. After all, wrote Ignatius in his *Letter to the Trallians*, Jesus

> was carried in the womb, even as we are, for the usual period of time; and was really born, as we also are; and was in reality nourished with milk, and partook of common meat and drink, even as we do.

Ignatius' observation that Jesus suckled at his mother's breasts aligns with Hirst's accentuation of *The Virgin Mother*'s breasts. As the concept of Jesus nursing at his mother's breast acquired theological significance, the subject became the focus of countless homilies (sermons), hymns, and poems. By the 7th century, artists took up the theme and images of the Virgin *lactans* (Latin, 'nursing') began to appear. The earliest examples are preserved in the cells of Egyptian monks, painted as aids to meditation. The image flourished for another 800 years until the Council of Trent suppressed it. Other important beliefs coalesced around Mary's breasts. For example, they betokened Mary's power of intercession: because Jesus drew life from Mary's breasts, he could not deny her requests. Milk from Mary's breasts also took on immense sanctity in the form of relics to which pilgrims flocked from all over Europe. In 1511, seeking the Virgin's aid for their infant son, King Henry VIII and Queen Katherine of Aragon travelled to the great English Marian pilgrimage shrine of Walsingham, whose high altar was crowned by a vial of Mary's milk.

The Virgin Mother may also disturb viewers because she is so young. UNICEF has declared that 'marriage before the age of 18 is a fundamental violation of human rights', yet *The Virgin Mother* looks scarcely old enough to have entered puberty. For better or worse, Christian tradition and actual 1st-century Jewish marital practice suggest that the historical Mary would have conceived Jesus at a very young age, younger even than the prototype for *The Virgin Mother*, Edgar Degas's beloved 1881 sculpture, *Little Dancer of Fourteen Years*. The youth of *The Virgin Mother* is also a reminder of the Immaculate Conception, reflecting the Council of Trent's mandate that Mary of the Immaculate Conception be a girl of 12 or 13. For Council members, Mary's youth constituted not just historical truth but a sign of her bodily purity. As anthropologists have shown, youth and virginity are often associated with visionary gifts of unmediated access to the divine. Notably, then, unlike the *Little Dancer*—or the *Miraculous Medal*—Mary's eyes are wide open as she gazes upward, as if her encounter with the angel Gabriel has alerted her to some new dimension of sight and sound.

The sheer size of Hirst's *The Virgin Mother* may also seem unusual because, excluding Byzantine apse mosaics, images of the Virgin Mary traditionally have ranged from miniature—like the *Miraculous Medal*—to slightly over life-sized. Nevertheless, *The Virgin Mother* recalls the enormous Mary statues erected in Catholic locales across the globe since the mid-20th century. Explanations for this phenomenon are complex, including the Virgin's close association with anti-Communism during the Cold War, but giant-sized Mary statues are often right-wing

11

declarations of resistance to Vatican II efforts to rein in what the Council deemed excessive devotion to the Virgin and, by extension, rejection of religious and political liberalization.

Size has always played a role in religious and secular visual propaganda. Art historians call this hierarchical scale: the bigger the figure the more powerful its subject. *The Virgin Mother*'s scale and title call to mind the ancient virgin goddess Athena and her colossal ivory and gold statue in the Parthenon of Athens. Athena's size reflected the ancient belief that gods and goddesses far exceeded humans in size. Every branch of Christianity insists that Mary is not a goddess, but this is a fine distinction that everyday piety often ignores. In her monumentality, *The Virgin Mother* conjures up not just ancient goddesses but Mary herself as the invincible virgin warrior who drove attackers from the walls of Constantinople in the 7th century and was hailed in the Greek Orthodox *Akathistos* hymn as 'our leader in battle and defender'.

These two artworks express the Marian contradiction between weakness and power as well as the complex history of Marian beliefs. Today the Virgin is still a role model for millions, but, 'alone of all her sex', as mother and virgin at the same time, the Virgin Mary is also a figure who, as feminists point out, real women can never hope to emulate. Feminists contend that devotion to the Virgin has encouraged Christian women and men to take a negative attitude toward the human body. At the same time, Liberation theology embraces the Virgin as one who fights injustice through her powers of intercession and is devoted to the poor in the here and now. Ultimately, Mary is the woman whose flesh and blood guarantees the foundations of Christian theology. So much from a girl first encountered ever so briefly in the Bible.

Chapter 2
Mary in the New Testament, history, and earliest Christianity

Any survey of the Virgin Mary and her role in Christianity necessarily begins with Mary in the New Testament, the earliest source to mention her. The New Testament is the essential starting point for Mary's place in Christianity, but only the starting point. This chapter will introduce two key factors in the development of Marian beliefs: the evolution of Christian doctrine over time and God's plan of salvation. Finally, while the New Testament provides the earliest information about Mary, we will see that it does not amount to very much. The chapter closes with an attempt to describe the real life—or, in historians' terms, the 'historical'—Mary based not just on the New Testament but also on relevant archaeological and historical data.

The New Testament: historical and literary perspectives

Christianity arose out of the life and ministry of Jesus of Nazareth, a Jew crucified around 30 CE by the Romans for sedition against the Roman empire, but whose followers claimed he had risen from the dead. For the first generation of what scholars call the Jesus Movement, Jesus's resurrection signalled the imminent end of the world. According to the Gospel of Mark (13:30, 26) Jesus promised his followers, 'This generation will not pass away' before they see 'the Son of Man coming in clouds with great power and glory'. What would be the point, then, of documenting the life of Jesus, much less planning for anything but the Last Judgement when Christ would return to earth? We can see this attitude in Paul's letters which pre-date the Gospels and which concentrate on Christ's death, resurrection, and Second Coming, but say nothing about Jesus's life, miracles, or teaching. Only when it became obvious that the 'End' was not yet near did Jesus's second-generation followers take up their pens to record the life of Jesus—with occasional references to his mother, Mary—in the Gospels of Matthew, Mark, Luke, and John. The four canonical (that is, approved as authoritative) Gospels subsequently joined twenty-three other documents written between 50 and 120 CE that were gathered together to become the New Testament.

The Christians who composed the New Testament Gospels knew nothing about modern 'objective' history writing. They followed ancient literary conventions that merged history and theology, the one influencing the other. For example, the stories of Jesus's birth in the Gospels of Matthew and Luke conform to the norms of Graeco-Roman biography in which a subject's future greatness is signalled by a remarkable birth and/or childhood. Each Gospel was also written in a different place and time, so Gospel stories are coloured by concerns of the author's time period and framed within ever-expanding oral traditions about Jesus. Finally, since Jesus in his lifetime seems never to have systematically explained who he was or what he meant to accomplish, each Gospel represents its author's attempt to work out what to believe about Jesus. The technical term for Christian thinking about Jesus's identity is Christology. Because each Gospel is informed by differing Christologies, each account of Jesus and, consequently, of Mary, differs.

The New Testament Gospels plus one verse in Acts of the Apostles are the only 1st-century sources that mention Mary at all, and she appears in only a few chapters. No texts written after the New Testament contain any additional historical information about

Mary. The many apocryphal documents (i.e. post-1st-century biblical-style writings of unknown authorship and disputed scriptural status) reflect what Christians were coming to believe about her, beliefs that split like a family tree into branches of varying vigour. These branches extend across two millennia and into the 21st century.

Missing Mary?

Before we look more closely at Mary in the New Testament, we must note that there are discontinuities between the scriptural Mary of the New Testament and many Marian beliefs and doctrines that eventually developed within the Church (see Box 1). The opening chapters of Matthew and Luke narrate the story of Jesus's miraculous birth to the Virgin Mary in Bethlehem, but no other New Testament book alludes to Jesus's nativity at all. In the later chapters of Matthew and Luke, no one, Mary included, seems aware of anything remarkable about Jesus's birth. The primary focus of the New Testament books is on human salvation through the resurrection of Jesus the Messiah (or 'Christ', Greek for the Hebrew term, 'Messiah').

Some scholars suggest that the New Testament's apparent overall indifference to the circumstances of Jesus's birth or to Mary herself indicates that in the Jesus Movement's first decades, most of Jesus's followers assumed that he was born just like everyone else. This may explain, for example, Jesus's response in Luke 11 when a woman calls out, 'Blessed is the womb that bore you and the breasts that nursed you!' and Jesus corrects her, 'Blessed rather are those who hear the word of the Lord and obey it.' According to this theory, Matthew's and Luke's nativity stories may initially have had limited circulation and came about when the Gospel-writers combined oral traditions about Jesus with biblical and Graeco-Roman story patterns. In the middle of the 1st century, a generation before the appearance of Mark, the earliest Gospel (written around 70), the apostle Paul was explaining in

Box 1 What Christians believe about Mary today

Catholic and Orthodox Christians differ from Protestants in how they interpret Gospel references to Jesus's brothers and sisters. This difference exemplifies doctrinal disagreements about Mary that, in turn, arise from differences in how the three main Christian denominations approach the Bible.

The Catholic and Orthodox Churches consider the Bible to be the primary source of theological doctrine, but also ascribe doctrinal authority to the tradition (or teaching) of the Church. This appeal to church tradition is based in part on Jesus's promise in John 14:17–18 that God would send 'another advocate, to be with you forever ... This is the spirit of truth.' Because the advocate came to be understood as the Holy Spirit, Catholics and Orthodox believe that the Holy Spirit is continually present in the Church, providing guidance and inspiration. Church tradition is viewed as this divine guidance, articulated over the centuries by church authorities. (Most) Protestants, on the other hand, espouse the principle of *sola scriptura* (Latin, 'scripture only') demanded by Protestant reformers in the 16th century. In their view, anything not commanded or attested in the Bible cannot be doctrine.

Catholics and Orthodox profess Mary's perpetual virginity on the basis of tradition, that is, authoritative church teaching inspired by the Holy Spirit. Protestants disagree, objecting that 'it is not in the Bible'. Catholics and Orthodox pray to saints for intercession. (Most) Protestants do not pray to saints because no one in the Bible prayed to a saint. Based on the Bible and on church tradition, Catholics profess the Seven Sacraments (rituals that impart divine grace): Baptism, Confirmation, Eucharist (Holy Communion), Holy Orders, Marriage, Penance (Reconciliation/Confession), and Anointing the Sick. (Most) Protestants accept only Baptism and Eucharist because only they occur in the Bible.

Catholics profess Four Marian Dogmas (officially prescribed belief): Mary's Divine Motherhood, Perpetual Virginity, Immaculate Conception, and Assumption. Orthodox belief overlaps with Catholic to a considerable degree, although the Orthodox reject the term Immaculate Conception and explain Mary's sinlessness according to different reasoning. Of these four dogmas, Protestants acknowledge only Mary's divine motherhood, again, because the Bible says the Virgin Mary gave birth to Jesus the Saviour.

letters to churches what he believed about Jesus. Paul makes no reference to Jesus's birth or to Mary. If the married brothers of Jesus mentioned by Paul in 1 Corinthians 9:5 were full siblings, then Mary could have been a grandmother. On the other hand, because the Greek word for brothers could sometimes mean half-siblings, from as early as the 2nd century Jesus's brothers and sisters mentioned in the Gospels would usually be identified as Joseph's offspring from an earlier marriage that had left him a widower. This tradition is maintained by Catholics and Orthodox (see Box 1).

In the Gospels the adult Jesus projects a fairly aloof attitude toward his mother and siblings, though he shows concern for his mother in John's account of the Crucifixion. An ancient Christian creed preserved in a speech by Jesus's disciple Peter (Acts 2:22–4) describes only the adult Jesus. In the same vein, the oldest extant Christian hymn (Philippians 2:6–11) stresses Jesus's incarnation with no allusion to unusual birth: Jesus 'was in the form of God' but was 'born in human likeness' and 'in human form'. Paul's New Testament letters suggest he has no knowledge of or interest in Jesus's birth or, indeed, his miracles and parables. Elsewhere in the New Testament, when a follower of Paul complained that Christians showed too much interest in 'myths and endless genealogies that promote speculations' (Timothy 1:4), the writer may have been repudiating nativity stories and genealogies of Jesus like those in Matthew and Luke.

However, any apparent indifference in the New Testament to Jesus's birth and the Virgin Mary was soon swept aside. The virgin birth became an essential belief in most Christian circles. We see this in the early 2nd-century *Letter to the Ephesians* by Ignatius of Antioch who declared that there were 'three mysteries hidden from the Prince of this age: the virginity of Mary and her birth-giving, together with the death of the Lord'. Christians now began to interpret the New Testament in the firm belief that all the New Testament writers took Mary's virginal conception of Jesus for granted, too. In this way, developing Marian beliefs were rooted in scriptural interpretation.

Evolving Christianity

Christianity is grounded in the Bible, but what Christians today take for granted about their religious beliefs evolved over centuries of reflection and debate. From archaeological discoveries and new approaches to ancient texts—which include the books of the New Testament—scholars now know that in early Christianity (the 1st to 4th centuries) people who professed faith in Jesus maintained a surprising diversity of beliefs and practices, not just about Jesus but also about his mother, Mary. The first official definition of Christian beliefs, the Nicene Creed, only appeared in 325 after Christianity was decriminalized by the Roman Emperor Constantine (Box 2). Today, although Christians are divided into some 38,000 separate denominations, for the most part the Nicene Creed still unites them all.

But the Nicene Creed evolved, too. In 325 when the Creed first summarized universal Christian beliefs about Jesus, it did not mention Mary. The Creed affirmed only that Jesus 'was made

Box 2 Nicene Creed (Revision of 381)

I believe in one God,
the Father almighty,
maker of heaven and earth,
of all things visible and invisible.
I believe in one Lord Jesus Christ,
the Only Begotten Son of God,
born of the Father before all ages.
God from God, Light from Light,
true God from true God,
begotten, not made, consubstantial with the Father;
through him all things were made.
For us men and for our salvation
he came down from heaven,
and by the Holy Spirit was incarnate of the Virgin Mary,
and became man.
For our sake he was crucified under Pontius Pilate,
he suffered death and was buried,
and rose again on the third day
in accordance with the Scriptures.
He ascended into heaven
and is seated at the right hand of the Father.
He will come again in glory
to judge the living and the dead
and his kingdom will have no end.
I believe in the Holy Spirit, the Lord, the giver of life,
who proceeds from the Father;
who with the Father and the Son is adored and glorified,
who has spoken through the prophets.
I believe in one, holy, catholic and apostolic Church.
I confess one Baptism for the forgiveness of sins
and I look forward to the resurrection of the dead
and the life of the world to come. Amen.

man', an indication that church leaders were still working out the full theological significance of Jesus's birth and Mary's essential place in Christology. Fifty-five years later, in 381, the Nicene Creed was slightly revised to accommodate disputes over the vexing question of the Hypostatic Union, the Christological term for how the human and the divine combined in Jesus. It was at this point that the phrase 'and by the Holy Spirit was incarnate of the Virgin Mary' entered the Creed to emphasize that Jesus's humanity came from his mother, Mary.

New Testament Mary

What does the New Testament actually say about Mary? As historians do, let us examine her appearances in the order the books that mention her were written. As we have seen, Paul's letters were written first. The four gospels—Matthew, Mark, Luke, and John—were written a generation or more after Paul's letters. (This is obscured by the fact that the Gospels come before Paul's letters in the New Testament.) In chronological order, after Paul comes Mark, then Matthew, Luke, and finally, John. Taking the books in this order reveals a pattern consistent with each book's developing Christology. Beginning with Paul's letters and ending with John's Gospel, the moment when Jesus is recognized as divine—often signalled by the title 'Son of God'—shifts steadily earlier in time and Mary's role in Jesus's life expands.

Paul links the title 'Son of God' with Jesus's resurrection, writing that Jesus was 'declared to be Son of God...by resurrection from the dead' (Romans 1:40). Paul never mentions Mary and perhaps never knew about any miraculous birth, though at least two of Jesus's twelve apostles, Peter and John, were personally known to Paul and would presumably have informed him of this had they known of it. Paul simply says that Jesus was 'born of a woman' (Galatians 4:4), a common expression that meant Jesus had a mother like everyone else.

Mark says nothing about Jesus's birth either, but according to Mark, Jesus is declared the Son of God not at his Resurrection but at his baptism when a heavenly voice announces, 'You are my Son' (Mark 1:11). Unlike Paul, Mark knows something about Jesus's mother including her name. In Mark 3 Jesus returns to his hometown of Nazareth and his 'mother and his brothers' try to restrain him because the neighbours think Jesus has 'gone out of his mind'. Jesus then asks, '"Who are my mother and my brothers?" And looking at those who sat around him, he said, "Here are my mother and my brothers! Whoever does the will of God is my brother and sister and mother."' Later, in Mark 6:3, after hearing Jesus preach in the Nazareth synagogue, the scandalized townsfolk remark dismissively, 'Is this not the son of Mary and brother of James and Joses and Judas and Simon, and are not his sisters here with us?' This is the very first mention of Mary by name.

Matthew and Luke borrowed the two Nazareth episodes from Mark, although they left out the reference to madness. However, according to both Matthew and Luke Jesus becomes the Son of God not as an adult, as Mark claimed, but before birth, at his miraculous conception by Mary. In accordance with our pattern, in Matthew and Luke Mary assumes greater narrative weight, although more so in Luke than Matthew, who makes Joseph, not Mary, the protagonist in the nativity story. Matthew and Luke also provide genealogies for Jesus traced through Joseph, not Mary, and list King David and Abraham among Jesus's ancestors.

In Matthew it is to Joseph that the angel explains that Mary's perplexing pregnancy is 'from the Holy Spirit' (Matthew 1:20). Nothing further is reported of Jesus's nativity, and Mary is only mentioned by name once more in the story, when Magi ('wise men') follow the star to 'the house' in Bethlehem where they encounter 'the child with Mary his mother' (Matthew 2:9–11). It is Joseph who receives the angel's command to flee to Egypt from King Herod's baby-killers and later to return home.

In Luke, Mary says and does a lot more. Luke begins with the miraculous conception of John the Baptist by the elderly Zachariah and Mary's cousin Elizabeth. Jesus's even more incredible conception follows, with the angel Gabriel announcing Jesus's conception to Mary, a betrothed virgin of Nazareth. Mary hastens to visit her pregnant cousin Elizabeth, and the women's joyous meeting climaxes with Mary singing the *Magnificat*, so-called because the first word of the Latin text is *magnificat*, '[my soul] magnifies [the Lord]' (Luke 1:46). Here Mary's action recalls her namesake Miriam at the Exodus, who sang of God's triumph over the Pharaoh (Exodus 15: 20–21).

Joseph and Mary, 'who was expecting a child', journey to Bethlehem where they find 'no place for them at the inn' and Mary 'gave birth to her firstborn son' (Luke 2:1–7). They are visited by shepherds who find Jesus 'wrapped in bands of cloth and lying in a manger' (Luke 2:12). Luke describes Jesus's circumcision and sets two episodes in the Jerusalem temple, Judaism's most sacred place: Mary's post-partum Jewish purification ritual and, twelve years later, Joseph and Mary's discovery of their missing son teaching the elders in the Temple. Unusually for a biblical book, Luke provides a glimpse of Mary's interior life as she 'treasures' and 'ponders' events 'in her heart'.

Matthew and Luke agree with Mark in not including Mary among the women who witness the Crucifixion and Resurrection. In Acts 1 (attributed to Luke) Mary appears once more; after Jesus has ascended to heaven, 'Mary the mother of Jesus, as well as his brothers' gather to pray. Mary, although unnamed, seems also to be present for the descent of the Holy Spirit on Jesus's twelve disciples at Pentecost (Acts 2). This public moment recalls Mary's private experience in Luke when Gabriel's promise, 'The Holy Spirit will come upon you, and the power of the Most High will overshadow you' (1:35), comes to pass.

The Gospel of John, like the Gospel of Mark, provides no nativity story. John actually dispenses with earthly time altogether: in John 1, Jesus's divinity is in place even before God creates the universe. Jesus (called *logos*, Greek for 'word') 'was in the beginning with God'. Consistent with the Gospel of John's high Christology (i.e. stressing Jesus's divine aspects) the Gospel shies away from a mundane human phenomenon like childbirth. John 1:14 simply states, 'the Word [i.e. Jesus] became flesh'. Here we see the first articulation of the Christological concept of incarnation. Interestingly, the earliest translation of John into Syriac (the Aramaic dialect of eastern Christians) calls Jesus 'the only-begotten son, which is from the womb of the Father', explicitly distancing Jesus from association with human motherhood.

Nevertheless, in John, 'the mother of Jesus'—John never gives her name—appears in two momentous episodes unique to John's Gospel that mark the beginning and end of Jesus's ministry. During the Wedding at Cana in John 2 Mary helps bring about Jesus's first miracle when he turns water into wine. Thereafter, in contrast to the other Gospels, Mary accompanies her son in his travels. The second Marian episode in John, in marked distinction from the other Gospels, finds Mary at the Crucifixion. Looking down from the cross, Jesus commits Mary and the 'disciple whom he loved' to each other's care (John 19:29; later tradition identified him as John the Evangelist). In future centuries when Mary came to personify the Church, this scene was identified as the inauguration of the Church as a family united not by ties of blood but in the love of Christ.

Mary for Jews and Gentiles

Another perspective on Mary in the Gospels is gained by identifying themes in Matthew and Luke that underlie important Christian beliefs about Mary. This approach begins by acknowledging the hybrid origins of Christianity in both Judaism and Graeco-Roman culture. While Christianity was born Jewish, so to speak, the Jesus message spread rapidly, first among Jewish communities of the Roman empire and all but simultaneously, as we see from Paul's activities, among Graeco-Roman Gentiles. One indication of this rapid expansion beyond Jerusalem and Jesus's native Galilee is that the New Testament books were not written in Aramaic, the language of Jesus, Mary, and the disciples, but in Greek, the language of the eastern Roman empire. Let us consider how Jewish and Graeco-Roman religious thinking affects the portrayal of Mary first in Matthew, the most Jewish of the Gospels, and then in Luke, whose Gospel seems directed especially at Gentile Christians.

Matthew: God's plan of salvation

Matthew's story of Jesus's nativity, including Mary's part in it, was shaped by a type of Jewish Bible interpretation that became a linchpin of Christian theology. Jewish sages of the time believed that all of history, including the hoped-for appearance of the Jewish Messiah, conformed to a divine plan, God's plan of salvation, that could be discerned by careful, prayerful reading of scripture. Jewish belief in a coming Messiah, whom Jesus's earliest followers—all of them Jewish—identified as Jesus of Nazareth, was based on this Jewish approach to scripture. Indeed, it is the main reason Christianity did not 'throw out' the Jewish scriptures (renamed the 'Old Testament') even after Christians adopted the New Testament.

God's plan of salvation is the single most important conceptual framework for understanding the Virgin Mary in Christian theology, art, and devotion. Following the lead of Jewish sages who interpreted scripture as prophesying the Messiah, early followers of Jesus tended to believe that everything in the Jewish scriptures—every event, every character, every psalm, every prophet's speech—pointed to Jesus of Nazareth as the expected Jewish Messiah. In theological terms, then, Christians read the Old Testament as both blueprint and proof of God's plan of salvation: from the beginning of creation God planned to redeem humanity from sin by sending the Messiah, Jesus of Nazareth.

Paul (who was, after all, a Jew) used this type of Jewish interpretation to point out in Romans 1:2–4 that 'through his prophets in the holy scriptures' God had promised the 'gospel concerning his son'. For Paul, 'holy scriptures' were the Jewish scriptures. Luke says the resurrected Jesus also used this technique to teach his apostles: Jesus, 'beginning with Moses and all the prophets, interpreted to [the apostles] the things about himself in all the scriptures' (Luke 24:27). Following naturally from the conviction that the Jewish scriptures foreshadowed Jesus, Christians began to identify foreshadowings of Mary in the scriptures, too.

Matthew's very first verse alludes to God's plan: 'An account of the genealogy of Jesus the Messiah, the son of David, the son of Abraham.' In linking Jesus here with two of the most illustrious biblical ancestors of all, Matthew demonstrates that the Messiah whom God promised to the Jews is Jesus. As Abraham's descendant, Jesus's Jewish identity is established. Jesus's descent from King David is equally significant, since in Jesus's time many Jews expected their Messiah to come from David's bloodline. Remarkably, since women rarely figure in biblical genealogies, Jesus's family tree in Matthew names four biblical women; Tamar, the daughter-in-law of Judah, who was accused of prostitution (Genesis 38), Rahab the Canaanite prostitute (Joshua 2), Ruth the bold Moabite widow (the book of Ruth), and Bathsheba, the 'wife of Uriah', who committed adultery with King David (2 Samuel 11–12). Like the embarrassingly pregnant Mary in Matthew, whom Joseph wanted to send quietly away, each of these women, despite engaging in seemingly irregular sexual activity, is revealed to have acted according to God's divine plan. In portraying Mary this way, Matthew expresses what theologians since Paul have called the 'scandal' of the Gospel, that with Christ, established conventions—the political and social status quo—are set aside; God's plan surpasses human assumptions.

Matthew's case for Jesus as the fulfilment of God's plan becomes even more straightforward in the ensuing birth story as each episode is linked to a biblical quotation inserted to prove that the episode fulfils a Messianic prophecy from the scriptures. The first of these 'fulfilment quotations' relates directly to Mary. Matthew quotes the Greek translation of Isaiah 7:14 to explain that the Virgin Mary's miraculous conception of Jesus 'took place to fulfil what had been spoken by the Lord through the prophet: "Look, the virgin shall conceive and bear a son, and they shall name him Emmanuel"' (1:22–3). Christians would regularly invoke Isaiah 7:14 alongside Matthew and Luke's nativity stories as a major proof text. When opponents of Christianity correctly pointed out that the original Hebrew wording of Isaiah 7:14 used the word for 'young woman' and not 'virgin', Christians like Justin Martyr cleverly retorted that since Jews believed the Greek translation of the Bible had been divinely inspired, it must have been God who chose the Greek word for virgin in Isaiah 7.

Matthew's account of the nativity of Jesus was also indebted to Jewish *midrash*, creative biblical interpretation that provided additional stories about important biblical figures. Joseph's dream and Herod's fear of the newborn king of the Jews in Matthew are both indebted to midrashic stories of Moses, Matthew's favourite biblical 'foreshadower' of Jesus. Jewish Bible interpretation also includes a precedent for Mary as a virgin conceiving the son of God in Sarah, the mother of Isaac (whose near-sacrifice Christians interpreted as foreshadowing Jesus's Crucifixion). In *On the Cherubim* the 1st-century Jewish philosopher Philo of Alexandria refers to Sarah not only as 'conceiving a son when God beheld her by himself', but also to God making Sarah who 'before was a woman into a virgin again' to conceive Isaac.

Luke: God's plan of salvation in the Graeco-Roman world

Luke, too, situates Jesus within God's plan of salvation, and Luke's portrayal of Mary provides a good example of Luke's sophisticated biblical allusions. On the one hand, Matthew's Gospel never explains why God chose Mary, and in Luke 1:28 the angel Gabriel's salutation is equally uninformative. 'Greetings favoured one. The Lord is with you!' means essentially that Mary has been honoured by being chosen by God. On the other hand, in the ensuing conversation, Luke deftly depicts a polite girl whose question, 'How can this be, since I do not know a man?' (the literal Greek translation), shows a healthy degree of scepticism before she acquiesces to Gabriel's stunning declaration. More significantly, however, Mary's hesitancy is a conventional part of a biblical story pattern known as a 'call narrative' in which God (a) calls upon an unlikely person (in Mary's case, a girl) to perform a heroic task, (b) the person objects, (c) God overrules the objection, and (d) the chosen individual consents, because, as Gabriel reassures Mary, 'nothing will be impossible with God' (Luke 1:37). Mary's participation in this interchange links her to other initially unlikely biblical heroes chosen by God to advocate justice like Moses and Jeremiah. When Mary sings God's praises in the *Magnificat*, she quotes extensively from 1 Samuel 2, the joyous song of Hannah, mother of the prophet Samuel.

Saturated though it is with biblical language, the nativity story in Luke also resembles Graeco-Roman myths, particularly a late 1st-century BCE account of the hero Herakles (or Hercules) in the *Library of History* by Diodorus Siculus. Luke needed to 'translate' the distinctly Jewish meaning of 'son of god' into the very different, essentially genetic terms that 'son of god' implied to non-Jews in the Roman empire. Both Luke and Diodorus provide a genealogy and recount prophecies of the as-yet-unborn hero's greatness. Like Herakles, Jesus has a divine father and a mortal mother who is the chaste wife of a human husband. The birth of each child is preceded by that of a cousin whose public status initially overshadows his own. News of both boys' births in unexpectedly humble locations is met with 'amazement', a technical term in Graeco-Roman accounts of divine appearances. In adulthood, after performing superhuman deeds and enduring great suffering, both Jesus and Herakles become immortal, joining their divine father in heaven. And both writers show how the human and divine qualities of the parents come together in the child. In mirroring Jesus and Herakles, Luke was most likely capitalizing on audience familiarity with Herakles, whose worshippers could be found throughout the Roman empire, not least in the eastern Mediterranean and Syria-Palestine.

Revelation 12 and the celestial mother

Even though Mary doesn't appear in it, one additional New Testament book is pertinent to the Virgin Mary, albeit not in the sense its author originally intended. The last book of the New Testament, Revelation, dates to the end of the 1st century and includes visions of the end of the world. In one vision (12:1–2):

> A great portent appeared in heaven: a woman clothed with the sun, with the moon under her feet, and on her head a crown of twelve stars. She was pregnant and was crying out in birth pangs, in the agony of giving birth.

The author here is using the common biblical metaphor of Israel as a woman. This motif has been interwoven in the book of Revelation with mythological references from multiple ancient cultures including the moon symbolism of the mother goddess Artemis/Diana, whose cult was strong in Asia Minor where Revelation was probably written. The twelve stars refer to the twelve tribes of Israel and originate in the dream of Joseph, son of Jacob/Israel in Genesis 37:9. All this 'Israel' symbolism reflects the early Christian claim that Christians, not the Jews, were the true Israel and the rightful heirs to God's covenant with Abraham.

In the 4th century, Epiphanius of Salamis compared Mary to Revelation's 'woman clothed in the sun', a logical extension of the common belief that Mary symbolized the Church, the mother of Christians. The identification of Mary with the 'woman clothed in the sun' gained traction as popular devotion to Mary increasingly ascribed supernatural qualities to her. Eventually, the celestial woman in Revelation influenced how Christians visualized Mary's Assumption into heaven and influenced the iconography of the Virgin Mary as the Immaculate Conception, thereby providing a scriptural anchor for two popular Marian dogmas.

The historical Mary

Finally, what can history tell us about the real-life Mary? In some ways, very little. In the mid-1970s a joint Roman Catholic and Protestant Lutheran study concluded that the virginal conception of Jesus by Mary could not be proved as historical fact based on modern scientific methods of verification. Beyond the New Testament, however, archaeological and historical data about Mary's 1st-century Palestinian world allow us to engage in some informed speculation about the woman who was Jesus's mother.

Mariam was the name most frequently given to 1st-century Jewish girls, apparently in memory of the prophet Miriam, Moses' sister. (Originally, both Moses and Miriam were Egyptian name-elements respectively meaning 'son of' and 'beloved'.) As with most people in the Gospels, Mary's parents are not named. In Mary's youth her northern Jewish province of Galilee was ruled by Rome's vassal, King Herod the Great (37–4 BCE), and Luke's Gospel plausibly situates Jesus's birth during the long reign of the Roman Emperor Augustus (27 BCE–14 CE). An hour's walk from Nazareth was the city of Sepphoris, where a Jewish revolutionary attack in 4 BCE drew harsh reprisals by the Roman authorities. Mary and her family could not have been unaffected to some degree by the repercussions of this clash between Romans and Galilean Jews so nearby.

The Bible rarely describes anyone's appearance, and this is true for Mary, too. The earliest description of Mary comes from a 9th-century *Life of Mary* by Epiphanius the Monk. He claims she had 'a light complexion, light brown hair and eyes, black eyebrows, a straight nose, a long face and long hands and fingers'. His description follows the conventions of Byzantine icons, but is perfectly conceivable for an eastern Mediterranean girl.

Living poor in the rural village of Nazareth, Mary, like her neighbours, would not have been able to read or write. Jewish traditions were learned from the daily practices of Jewish household religion, including dietary rules, and from the yearly festal cycle. These would have fostered a distinctive Jewish identity in the face of Roman occupation. Her days may have begun and ended with the recital of the *Shema* ('Hear O Israel, the Lord is our God, the Lord alone...'; Deuteronomy 6:4–9), and after each menstrual cycle she most likely purified herself by full immersion in a *mikveh* or ritual bath. In addition to household duties, she may have wandered the surrounding hills in bare feet, tending the occasional sheep or goat that peasant families might own. When Mary's parents arranged her marriage to Joseph, he would have been in his twenties or thirties, the customary age of marriage for Jewish men. Matthew 13:55 says Jesus's father was a *tekton*, a Greek word usually translated 'carpenter', but which applied more broadly to wood-workers, masons, builders, and even teachers.

Since 1st-century Jewish girls married at the onset of puberty, Mary would have married Joseph at 12 or 13, becoming a mother some nine months later. The four Gospels strongly imply that after Jesus, Mary bore additional sons and daughters, although as we have already seen, this is not the Catholic or Orthodox understanding. Matthew's Gospel (Matthew 1:25) says that Joseph refrained from sexual intercourse with Mary until after Jesus was born. Given the era's 30 per cent infant mortality rate and the high probability of death in childbirth, a living mother with so many surviving children would impress her neighbours as conspicuously blessed by God.

Joseph's absence from the Gospel accounts of the adult Jesus's ministry has suggested to scholars that by this time Mary was a widow. In Acts, after Jesus's death she belongs to the community of Jesus followers in Jerusalem. The leader of the community was another of Mary's sons, James, one of the brothers of Jesus named in the Gospels and referred to as such by Paul. Like all Jesus's followers whose faith survived the Crucifixion, Mary would still have considered herself Jewish when she died. Although Mary's death is recounted in apocryphal texts, there is no historical evidence for when or where this occurred.

Chapter 3
Mary after the Gospels: new stories and evolving doctrine

Beliefs about the Virgin Mary did not develop in a linear trajectory, and it took centuries for Christians to arrive at all of the Marian doctrines that are part of Christianity today, among them her sainthood, her perpetual virginity, and her intercession in heaven for devotees on earth. In fact, scholars acknowledge that a lot remains mysterious about how different communities expressed their devotion to Jesus in the 2nd to the 4th centuries before any single 'brand' of Christianity won out and before Christians' ideas about Mary eventually coalesced around key Marian doctrines.

Archaeological evidence for the lives of any Christians, ordinary or elite, could help with the gaps in our knowledge about Mary in this period, but little exists before the 5th century. What exists is mostly funerary; early images of Mary appear on a few 3rd-century Roman catacomb frescos and burial slabs that depict the Adoration of the Magi (Figure 3). Mary, however, was not the focal point of these scenes; rather, Christians saw the coming of the Magi as God's signal that Gentiles, symbolized by Magi 'from the east', honoured Jesus. Jesus's sovereignty was still the theme of Pope Leo the Great's Epiphany sermon of 450 when he preached: 'In the three Magi let all people worship the author of the universe; and let God be known not in Judea alone, but in all the world.' Yet even before Pope Leo preached his sermon, ideas about

3. Adoration of the Magi, Balaam, and star; detail, epitaph of Severa, Catacombs of Priscilla, Rome. Late 3rd century.

Mary had developed to the point that the Virgin now symbolized the Church as a whole. Christians saw in the Adoration of the Magi not just the world acclaiming Jesus as Lord but also the world offering allegiance to the Church as a sacred institution, personified by Mary.

Lacking material evidence (aside from funerary art), most information about early Christian beliefs relative to Mary comes from texts: writings in Latin or Greek by the Church Fathers, who were credited with laying the theological foundations of Christianity; apocryphal texts, especially the *Protevangelium of James*, which centres on Mary; and other Christian writings, often in languages like Syriac (a form of Aramaic) and Coptic (the language of Egyptian Christians). Taken together, they reveal the swirl of ideas that characterized early Christianity generally and affected the Virgin specifically.

This chapter considers a time period when Christianity could sometimes seem like a religious free-for-all, with Mary featuring—or not—in remarkably varied ways. By the middle of the 5th century, however, the Virgin Mary's unique and lasting place in Christian piety alongside the closely allied belief in the spiritual superiority of bodily virginity had become established features of mainstream Christianity.

Church Fathers and Mary

Until the 5th century, the Church Fathers kept within fairly narrow parameters in their writings about Mary. Before 431, when the Council of Ephesus approved the formal Marian title *Theotokos* (Greek, 'One who gives birth to God' or 'God-bearer'), Mary figured in discussions by Church Fathers not on her own account but for reasons of Christology. In other words, early church authorities found that thinking about Mary helped them to work out what to believe about Jesus. Mary became part of the intense speculation about Jesus's incarnation and the hypostatic union because Jesus's humanity depended on his human mother. Church Fathers also broadened Justin's and Irenaeus' identification of Mary as the New Eve in God's plan of salvation, the essential conceptual framework for Marian theology. They did not, however, attribute any miracle-working or intercessory powers to her. As late as the 6th century, a Coptic theologian ridiculed the idea that Mary could be a 'mighty power in the heavens'.

The Church Fathers' views of Mary were overwhelmingly positive. After all, God chose her to be the mother of Jesus. But circumstances could sometimes dictate how a Church Father referred to Mary. Prominent admirers of the Virgin Mary could sometimes go negative. At one point in his commentary on the Gospel of Matthew, Jerome (late 4th century) called Mary a symbol of the Synagogue, in other words, a symbol of unbelieving Jews; here Jerome was repeating an opinion expressed in the 3rd century by Tertullian. At the Council of Ephesus in 431 Cyril of

Alexandria took the lead in promoting Mary as *Theotokos*, yet in Cyril's commentary on the Gospel of Luke, he agreed with Origen, who a century earlier had stated that Mary lacked faith at the Crucifixion.

There are problems, however, with reconstructing the earliest Marian beliefs based solely on the Church Fathers, Christological debates, and declarations at Ephesus. First, the Council of Ephesus did not officially declare Mary *Theotokos*, even though the title gained conciliar approval and Marian veneration notably gained momentum after 431. Second, the term 'Church Fathers' denotes a limited perspective. Church Fathers such as Ignatius, Irenaeus, Tertullian, and Jerome were elite men, and it was their writings that were ultimately judged to be orthodox and authoritative; as such they were preserved and copied while many once-revered works would be rejected as heterodox. At the same time, in their own lifetimes the supposed authority of the orthodox Church Fathers was no guarantee that other theologians or the common people agreed with them. The search for Mary's place in early Christianity must cast a wider net, beyond the Church Fathers to the more diverse record preserved in the apocrypha, and other texts.

Christian diversity

In 325, Emperor Constantine convened the Council of Nicaea to resolve theological disputes that were causing violent confrontations between his Christian subjects. For Constantine, unity of empire required unity of religious belief amongst his empire's widely spread churches. Under Constantine, as Christian leaders were pressured by the Emperor to assert uniform belief within the Church, Christian writings that did not hew to the evolving orthodox line were considered heterodox and subject to suppression. Bishop Athanasius' warning to a group of monks is typically ferocious:

let us...take care not to read the books composed by these defiled heretics, atheists, and truly irreverent people, so that we ourselves may not become disobedient to the Lord.

Athanasius' polemic was aimed at books that numerous Christian communities had long accepted as legitimate, including the apocryphal *Protevangelium of James*, which will be discussed below. Christian writings suppressed by the combined pressure of emperors and bishops were often lost, although many apocryphal texts survived, sometimes because translations into other languages escaped the culling. Many of these texts preserve clues to early Christian beliefs about the Virgin Mary before the 5th century, at which point a more unified Church expressed increasing devotion to Mary. Happily, portions of lost works can still be found as quotations in the writings of the Church Fathers and, in some cases, entire books have come to light through archaeological discoveries and from literary 'excavations' in ancient monastery libraries.

Some perspectives on Mary in these early Christian writings are familiar today; others would ultimately be rejected and/or forgotten. A case in point is an early apocryphal narrative describing the end of Mary's life, an event known as the *Koimesis* (Greek) or *Dormition* (Latin)—both terms mean falling asleep. In it, Mary confesses that she fears death because she once sinned, an idea also expressed in some 2nd- and 3rd-century texts. By the mid-4th century, though, we find Ephraim of Syria articulating what became basic Christian doctrine until the Reformation: that Mary was sinless. Ephraim explained that at the moment the Holy Spirit overshadowed Mary to conceive Jesus, she became baptized and freed of original sin. As much as Jesus's own baptism, it was Mary's baptism at the Annunciation by the Holy Spirit that informed the Syriac view of baptism; every Christian at the moment of baptism was just like Mary: overshadowed by the Holy Spirit, filled with Christ, and freed from original sin.

New Eve in the plan of salvation

One theme which Church Fathers and numerous other Christian sources enthusiastically embraced and expanded upon relates directly to God's plan of salvation: Mary as the New Eve. Paul had explained in 1 Corinthians 15:22 that Jesus undid the sin of Adam: 'for as all die in Adam, so all will be made alive in Christ'. Paul then deployed a classic Christian argument based on the plan of salvation. First, Paul gives a biblical quotation from Genesis: 'Thus it is written [in Genesis], "The first man, Adam, became a living being."' Then Paul explains that in this Bible verse the 'first man, Adam' foreshadowed Jesus, 'the last Adam [who] became a life-giving spirit' (1 Corinthians 15:45). In other words, Jesus is the new Adam who reverses the consequences of the first Adam's sin. The idea of a new Adam seemed to beg the question of a 'new Eve', and in the century after Paul this concept made its first appearance in writings by Justin Martyr and Irenaeus of Lyons.

In his *Dialogue with Trypho*, Justin Martyr drew a parallel between two biblical virgins, Eve in Genesis and Mary in Luke, to crown his proof that the 'scriptures' (the Old Testament) prophesied the coming of Jesus. Justin wrote,

> For Eve, who was a virgin…having conceived the word of the serpent, brought forth…death. But the Virgin Mary received faith and joy when the angel Gabriel announced the good tidings to her that the Spirit of the Lord would come upon her,….And by her has [Jesus] been born, to whom we have proved so many Scriptures refer.

The writings of these two 2nd-century Church Fathers set the stage for what would become an immensely productive Marian theological and iconographic tradition (see Figure 6). Jerome's statement from the 4th century is typical: 'Death came through Eve, but life has come through Mary' (*Epistle* 22.21). In the 7th-century Greek *Akathistos* hymn, Mary is hailed as the

'Redemption of the Tears of Eve'. Latin-speaking Christians found evidence of God's plan by noting that when Eve's Latin name, '*Eva*', is reversed, it becomes '*Ave*' ('Hail'), Gabriel's greeting to Mary, as if Eve were turned back the right way round. Latin poets loved this, as for instance in the refrain of a popular medieval carol, *Nova! Nova! Ave fit ex Eva!* ('News! News! *Ave* comes from *Eva*').

The beginnings of Marian intercession

Many Christians have found and continue to find profound solace in praying to Mary, certain in their faith that she will intercede for them with Christ in heaven. Yet Marian intercession was not actually something that the earliest Christians practised, and it took hold unevenly across time and space. Christians prayed to saints for aid and miracles, but Mary was not—at first— considered a saint. As neither a martyr nor an archangel Mary was not someone to pray to or dedicate churches to until the late 4th or early 5th century when the cult of saints had expanded to include her. Among early Christians, the pre-eminent female martyr-saint and miracle-worker was not the Virgin Mary but the virgin preacher Thecla. Her shrines in Asia Minor and Egypt drew pilgrims from all over the Byzantine empire seeking blessings and miraculous healing. Unlike Thecla, Mary lacked a dedicated pilgrimage shrine until the later 5th century when pilgrims began visiting a site in Jerusalem identified as Mary's (empty) tomb.

Mary's lack of influence over her son is vividly apparent in the 2nd-century apocryphal *Infancy Gospel of Thomas*. She stands helplessly by while her little boy wields deadly superpowers against neighbours who have annoyed him. No one in the story asks his mother to intervene with Jesus. During the Wedding at Cana (John 2), Jesus turns water into wine after Mary points out to him, 'They have no wine'; but unlike medieval interpreters, Church Fathers did not point out Marian intercession at Cana.

Rather, they worried over Jesus's brusque reaction to his mother, 'Woman, what concern is that to you and to me? My hour has not yet come.' Most concluded that Jesus was rebuking his mother for speaking out of turn and interfering; he would have helped out without her nudging him. Until recently, evidence that Christians sought Marian intercession as early as the 3rd century was claimed for a papyrus fragment in Manchester's John Rylands Library; the document is inscribed in Greek with a well-known Marian intercessory prayer known most commonly under its Latin name, *Sub Tuum Praesidium* ('Under your Protection'). Now, however, this 3rd-century dating has been revised to the 7th or 8th century, by which time Marian intercession was well established.

Devotion to Mary and the belief in her intercession developed gradually out of the practice of venerating martyrs, saints, apostles, and angels. For example, in the 3rd century a group of Christians with heterodox affinities sought intercession from a heavenly consortium that included Mary, the archangel Michael, and the apostles. Scattered 4th- and early 5th-century sources suggest that at least some Christians whose religious beliefs and practices anticipated the orthodox mainstream were seeking Mary's aid. An oration by Gregory of Nazianzus tells the story of a devout virgin who prayed to Jesus but also to Mary, whom she invoked as a sympathetic fellow-virgin, to rescue her from a seducer.

Hymns sung in the churches of Jerusalem, possibly from the early 5th century, ask Mary to 'intercede for the salvation of our souls'. Additional evidence for Christians seeking intercession from Mary, saints, and angels as a group may be found in healing spells on magical amulets from Egypt (Figure 4). A 5th-century spell written on behalf of a woman named Joannia calls on Christ to

... put to flight every fever-heat and every kind of chill ... and every evil, on account of the prayers and entreaties of our mistress, the

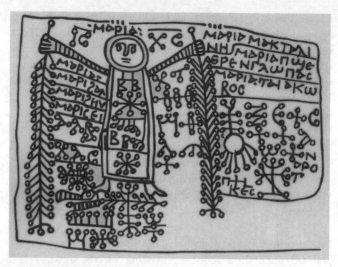

4. Coptic 'Magic Spell of Mary and the Angels', detail, 11th century (P. Heidelberg Inv. Copt 685 sheet 5). Mary is surrounded by magic rings, letters, and words; above Mary's head is written 'Maria', along with other Mary names including Mary Magdalene; an example of the composite Mary.

Theotokos, and of the glorious archangels and of John, the holy and glorious apostle...and all the saints.

Churches dedicated to all these holy figures, including 'Saint Mary', were among the forty churches in the Egyptian town of Oxyrhynchus, where the amulet was created. In the Holy Land, the Kathisma Church between Jerusalem and Bethlehem was probably erected in Mary's honour in the 5th century, possibly as an alternative to Bethlehem as the site of Jesus's birth. By the 6th century in Egypt, churches of St Mary were outnumbering those of other saints, including Thecla. It is now clear that Marian intercession was gaining acceptance before the Council of Ephesus in 431 and as of the 7th century was normative.

'My Mother the Holy Spirit'

As we have seen, Mary's motherhood of Jesus was a key factor in Christian attempts to wrap their minds around the complexities of Jesus's nature. Part of the thinking, preserved in some apocryphal texts, centred on the question of who Jesus's 'real' mother actually was. One answer was that Jesus's mother was the Holy Spirit. Before the 5th century, for Syriac-speaking Christians, the Trinity consisted of God the Father, Jesus the Son, and a female Holy Spirit (the Syriac word for 'spirit' is grammatically feminine). In the 2nd-century *Gospel of Thomas* Jesus declares, 'My [human] mother gave me falsehood, but my true mother [the Holy Spirit] gave me life.' And in the *Gospel of the Hebrews* Jesus says, 'Even now my mother the Holy Spirit took me by one of my hairs and carried me away to the great mountain Tabor.' The *Gospel of Philip* makes this assumption, too, implying further that Jesus was originally born in the normal way to Mary and Joseph, then was reborn at his baptism through the combined power of the feminine Holy Spirit and God the Father.

The theme of divine motherhood resulted in some surprising instances of gender fluidity in early Christian writings. In the apocryphal *Secret Book of John*, Jesus materializes as an eloquent infant to the Apostle John, identifying himself as all three persons of the Trinity: 'I am the Father, The Mother, The Son.' Identifying the male person of Jesus in this text as 'Mother' aligns with another early Christian trend, associating feminine breastmilk language not with Mary, Jesus's mother, but with God. Thus 1 Peter 2:2–3 teaches, 'Like newborn infants, long for the pure, spiritual milk, so that by it you may grow into salvation, if indeed you have tasted that the Lord is good.' The most striking example of this is found in the 2nd-century *Odes of Solomon* 19:

> …because [God the Father's] breasts were full,
>
> and it was undesirable that his milk should be released without purpose.

The Holy Spirit opened her bosom,

and mixed the milk of the two breasts of the Father.

…The womb of the Virgin took (it),

and she received conception and gave birth.

For this poet, the Holy Spirit is female, but the milk is God's, and it is the power of this milk that allows Mary as well as all believing Christians to conceive Christ within them. Comparable gender fluidity affects Mary when later in the same *Ode* she is described as giving birth to Jesus 'as if she were a man, of her own will'.

By the 5th century, however, the Syriac Church was using exclusively male pronouns for the Holy Spirit and Christians no longer invoked the Holy Spirit as Jesus's mother. Devotion to Mary was growing and the plain sense of the nativity stories in the Gospels became the norm among Christians: Jesus was born to the Virgin Mary, a human and a virgin who conceived him miraculously and gave birth to him as a real baby.

Christology, Mary, and the Council of Ephesus

Four centuries after Jesus's Crucifixion the Church was still struggling to explain how Jesus combined divine and human natures, the problem the Council of Ephesus was called to grapple with in 431. The ancient city of Ephesus enjoyed illustrious apostolic links to Paul and John the Evangelist, and by the time of the council its temple of Artemis/Diana, once a wonder of the ancient world, had lain in ruins for thirty years. Church leaders convened in one of the earliest attested churches dedicated to Mary (the ruined Mary church tourists are shown in Ephesus today was built well after the council). The council's task was to determine whether the Virgin Mary's baby was human or divine. Was Mary rightly called *Christotokos* ('one who gives birth to Christ', i.e. a man) or *Theotokos* ('one who gives birth to God', *theos*)?

For close to a century, especially in Egypt where the title originated, Mary had been addressed as *Theotokos* with no complicated theological implications. Bishop Nestorius from Antioch in Syria complained that saying Mary gave birth to God—that she was *Theotokos*—erred in two ways. First, a normal human birth would compromise Jesus's divinity; thus, said Nestorius, 'I do not [believe in] a two or three months-old [baby] God...for Mary was a human being and it is impossible that God should be born of a human being.' Second, Nestorius contended that calling Mary *Theotokos* failed to acknowledge Jesus's fully human nature, the part contributed by his mother. The majority of attending bishops, led by Cyril of Alexandria, found Nestorius' approach, which split Christ's nature into two distinct elements, too intellectualist and confusing. They insisted more simply that Jesus enjoyed coexistent divine and human natures. The winning faction, led by Cyril, argued that Mary guaranteed Jesus's humanity, but also that Mary's role in the incarnation of Christ could not be separated from his divinity.

Aware of popular devotion to Mary, in defiance of Nestorius and the Syrian Church's resistance to what might be called 'goddess-language creep', Cyril was mindful of his Egyptian Christian constituency, especially women, who already addressed the Virgin Mary as 'Divine Mother'. Even more influential on the council's outcome was the Emperor's sister, Princess Aelia Pulcheria. An aristocratic woman and dedicated virgin, Pulcheria identified herself with the Virgin Mary, the archetypal independent virgin. She and her elite sisters were natural advocates for Mary's enhanced theological status. Empowered by their association with the Virgin, Pulcheria and her elite fellow virgins could wield considerable influence in church affairs. By the end of the council, the title *Theotokos* had become a theologically calibrated expression of Christology that acknowledged Mary's essential role in conceiving and giving birth to the incarnate Word of God. Women bearing torches greeted the bishops as they left the council, scattering perfumed water in their path to celebrate the triumph of the 'one who gives birth to God' and rejoicing in their advocate with Jesus in heaven.

The Council of Ephesus occurred when Mary's popularity was already swelling among ordinary Christians. In the previous century, churches in the east had begun celebrating a yearly Marian feast. Jerusalem honoured Mary's maternity on 15 August, and the Byzantine capital commemorated 'Mary who erased the sin of Eve' on 26 December. Many churches were also including Mary in the Synaxis, the list of saints and martyrs recited during the Eucharist. Twenty years after Ephesus, the Council of Chalcedon (451) affirmed Mary as *Aeiparthenos* (Greek, 'ever-virgin'), thus bringing the Church's elite in line with beliefs already cherished by ordinary Christians.

New stories: *Protevangelium of James*

Given the sparse information about Mary in the Gospels, it is hardly surprising that stories began to appear to fill in the Gospels' gaps. The 2nd-century *Protevangelium of James* provided answers to questions about Mary's parentage, childhood, and life with Joseph. A couple of centuries later Dormition stories began to proliferate about the end of her life.

Protevangelium means 'before the Gospels', appropriately enough since it is mostly a Marian narrative prequel to the Gospels. Like so many apocryphal texts, it claims to be written by a biblical figure, in this case Jesus's brother, James, but the actual author is in fact unknown. The story begins with the lead-up to Mary's miraculous birth in Jerusalem to a childless elderly couple, Anna (Hannah) and Joachim. As it follows the events of Mary's life, the *Protevangelium*'s focus remains firmly on her virginity and bodily purity. At 3 years old, Mary goes to live what is essentially a cloistered life of service in the Jerusalem Temple, eating only heavenly food delivered each day by an angel. The onset of puberty when Mary is 12 years old compels the priests to find a husband for her, and Joseph, an elderly widower, is selected by a miracle. Directly after the marriage, Joseph travels away for work; Mary stays at home spinning scarlet and purple thread for the Temple curtain.

In contrast to Luke's account, Mary has not one but two angelic encounters in the *Protevangelium*. First, while drawing water at a well, Mary hears the angel's greeting but sees nothing. Later, back in Joseph's house, while Mary is spinning, the angel appears to her and announces she will bear Jesus. When Mary goes into labour in a cave near Bethlehem the infant Jesus materializes at Mary's feet in a light so intense 'eyes could not bear it'. There follows a remarkable episode in which a sceptical healer named Salome performs a vaginal examination on Mary to prove that Mary remains a virgin. This is one of the earliest references to Mary's *postpartum* virginity. The episode echoes Doubting Thomas's inspection of Jesus's wounds and may have served to refute contemporary accusations that Jesus was the illegitimate son of an adulterous mother.

The *Protevangelium*'s stress on Mary's ritual and sexual purity guaranteed that her son Jesus was likewise undefiled by sexual contamination. The *Protevangelium* is also the earliest text to assign Davidic ancestry to Mary; if Mary, Jesus's mother, was also descended from David, then this resolved the dilemma presented by the Gospel genealogies that linked Jesus to King David through Joseph, Jesus's supposed foster-father. Along the same lines, Joseph's status in the *Protevangelium* as an elderly widower with adult children explained the brothers and sisters of Jesus mentioned in the Gospels as half-siblings, rather than as children born to Mary after Jesus.

Suspicions of heterodoxy as well as its divergences from the Gospels explain the *Protevangelium*'s designation by church authorities as non-canonical. Jerome's opposition to it, for example, was well known. The supernatural arrival of the newborn Jesus in a burst of light points to a divine, Docetic Jesus rather than a doctrinally orthodox human Jesus. An early version of the *Protevangelium* may also have described Mary acting in some ritual—even priestly—capacity during her time in the Temple, and this, too, would have seemed problematic as Christianity began to reject older traditions of women leaders in the Church.

Canonical or not, the *Protevangelium of James* is the early Christian text with the greatest influence on Mariology. The Orthodox Church has always treated it with respect, reading it as a mystical meditation on the *Theotokos*. The western Church condemned it but did not prevent popular stories based on the *Protevangelium* from being told. Most Marian doctrines, in fact, can be traced back to it, and some of the earliest annual Marian feasts—the Conception of Mary, the Nativity of Mary, and Mary's Entrance into the Temple—commemorate events recounted in the *Protevangelium*, not the Bible. Soon after 800 the western Church adopted readings from this apocryphal text into the liturgy for the Feast of the Virgin's Nativity, and portions of the *Protevangelium* were incorporated into a Latin work with the lengthy title, the *Book About the Origin of the Blessed Mary and the Childhood of the Saviour*, which was attributed to Matthew (today it has a shorter name, the *Gospel of Pseudo-Matthew*).

The *Protevangelium* also was a huge influence on Christian art. One of the earliest images of the Virgin Mary appears on the 3rd-century baptistry wall at Dura Europos in eastern Syria. In a scene suggestive of the *Protevangelium*'s account of Mary hearing an angel's voice while drawing water, Mary is leaning over a well. This anticipates the fact that in the ensuing centuries many of the most popular Marian images were based on the *Protevangelium* rather than the Gospels. This is particularly true of Annunciation scenes, where Mary is either drawing water or spinning (see Figure 10, Chapter 5).

New stories: the Dormition

As for the end of Mary's life, Christians had proposed a variety of scenarios for her ultimate fate by the time Epiphanius of Salamis catalogued them in the later 4th century:

> The holy virgin may have died and been buried—her falling asleep was with honor…Or she may have been put to death—as scripture says, 'And a sword shall pierce through her soul'…Or she remained alive…No one knows her end.

The first story in Epiphanius' list clearly describes the Marian Dormition ('falling asleep') tradition. Now that many Christians considered Mary a saint, the term 'dormition' was a natural one to apply to her since it was already the Christian word for the end of a saint's life.

Dormition accounts such as the 5th-century *Book of Mary's Repose* or the later Latin *Transitus of Pseudo-Melito* can be quite different, but they all place Mary in Jerusalem when she learns that her end has come. Around her gather the apostles individually transported on a private cloud from their missions all over the world. The Archangel Michael and/or Jesus descends from heaven to supervise the final disposition of Mary's body and soul. Jesus receives Mary's soul while her body, washed by faithful virgins, is laid on a bier for the apostles to carry to her tomb. Neighbourhood Jews attack Mary's body during the funeral procession and when one of them reaches out to topple the bier, his offending hand falls off; once the Jew converts, however, his hand is restored. At the end, angels accompany Mary's soul up to heaven.

Dormition stories are the basis for western Christianity's celebration of the Assumption of Mary to heaven (declared as Catholic dogma in 1950) and the corresponding, but not identical, Orthodox celebration of *Koimesis*.

The Dormition and priestly Mary

Early Dormition traditions also constitute one of the richest sources for descriptions of female religious leadership in early Christianity, often portraying Mary and other women performing priestly, ritual tasks. In a Coptic account of the Dormition, Mary goes 'forth with the Apostles to preach' after Jesus's Ascension to heaven. Later, in Jerusalem at the end of her life, Mary meets with the apostles and they 'did as Mary ordered them: they prayed and prostrated themselves upon the earth'. Some versions refer to Mary burning incense, healing, and exorcizing demons.

Other early writings also treat Mary as a liturgical leader, performing tasks later associated only with male priests. In the 3rd-century *Questions of Bartholomew* Mary joins with the apostles and although she tries to defer to Peter as the 'chief' apostle, Peter and the rest insist Mary 'be the leader in the prayer'. Arms upraised, Mary praises God at length, and later 'with Mary they offered the Eucharist'. A description of Mary as a liturgical leader is also found in the earliest *Life of Mary*, a text that survives in a few old-Georgian manuscripts. This *Life of Mary* has been dated as early as the 7th century but is more likely 10th century. It includes an account of the Last Supper shared by both male and female disciples of Jesus. Mary is the women's teacher, officiating alongside Jesus as he authorizes both men and the women as ministers.

Such texts are not historical evidence that Mary was a leader during Jesus's ministry. Rather, they are evidence of the development of devotion to Mary; she is not yet an object of Christian devotion, but her religious authority far outstrips her relatively lowly status in the Gospels. By portraying Mary, a woman, performing liturgical actions, the texts indicate that some early Christian communities considered the presence of women in leadership roles a matter of course and not of controversy.

Although after Nicaea (325) texts like *Questions of Bartholomew* and Dormition narratives were condemned, nevertheless, the tradition of Mary as a religious authority persisted in eastern and western art and miracle tales. Byzantine church mosaics between the 6th and 11th centuries sometimes show Mary raising her arms in the orant (praying) position and equipped with either a pallium (a long strip of cloth bearing a cross worn by priests at the Eucharist) or maniple (a white eucharistic cloth). St Sofia Cathedral in Kyiv features a monumental 11th-century apse mosaic (Figure 5) with an orant Mary wearing a maniple tucked prominently into her belt. Directly below her is the altar where the Eucharist is celebrated. In the west, one of the songs in Spanish King Alfonso X's 13th-century *Cantigas* describes Mary administering the Easter Eucharist, and a 15th-century Missal (text of the Mass) shows her distributing communion wafers plucked from Eden's Tree of Life (Figure 6). Broadly speaking, when an image of the Madonna and Child appears above the altar in a church, Mary, no less than the priest, can be said to administer the Eucharist; where Mary offers her son, Jesus, the priest offers Jesus in the form of the consecrated host.

Surviving visual and textual portrayals of Mary praying and supervising at the Eucharist provide a historical counterweight to the Marian persona promoted by orthodox authorities like Athanasius, who in his *First Letter to Virgins* (346) praised Mary as the model virgin because Mary was not 'at all acquainted with the streets; rather, she remained in her house being calm...she did not acquire eagerness to look out the window, rather to look at the Scriptures...and prayed to God privately'. Athanasius has no problem with Mary as a solitary female reader of scripture, but he does not approve of her as a teacher with authority or special knowledge. This is the same Athanasius we saw earlier denouncing apocryphal texts, precisely the category of writings that preserve accounts of Mary's active leadership and which contradict his own characterization of Mary essentially as a cloistered virgin.

5. Orant (praying) Virgin, 11th century, apse mosaic, Cathedral of St Sofia, Kyiv, Ukraine.

The Virgin Mary and Mary Magdalene

The Virgin Mary's name has until recently been conspicuously absent from studies of female leadership in early Christianity. However, new awareness of texts and images like the ones considered here in which the Virgin Mary is a religious leader may stimulate some rethinking about another Mary, Mary Magdalene. Western Christianity's portrayal of Mary Magdalene as a prostitute was a fabrication of Pope Gregory in 691 and has since

6. *The Tree of Death and Life*, Berthold Furtmeyr (1489), detail, Munich, Bayerische Staatsbibliothek. Mary as the New Eve, accompanied by an angel, distributes Eucharist wafers from the Tree of Life; Eve, accompanied by a demon, distributes death-fruit via the snake from the same tree doubling as the Tree of Death. Adam asleep at the base of the tree alludes to the New Adam, Christ, and his salvific death on the cross, the new Tree of Life.

been repudiated by the Vatican. In contrast, eastern Christians have always honoured the Magdalene as 'Equal to the Apostles'. In their search for an early Christian feminist role model, 20th-century feminist theologians have often overlooked the Virgin Mary, uncritically taking for granted the stereotypical submissive Mary and thus dismissing her as a potential image of female Christian leadership. Among modern scholars and theologians, the model early Christian female leader has been Jesus's disciple Mary Magdalene. The apocryphal *Gospel of Philip*, for example, famously portrays Mary Magdalene as a religious authority who teaches the apostles and is acknowledged by them as Jesus's favourite.

Scholars have tended to identify any figure called Mary who acts with authority in early Christian texts as Mary Magdalene, even when the name Magdalene is absent. In question is whether the name 'Mary' might refer to the Virgin Mary instead. This ambiguity has even given rise to a scholarly tag: the 'muddle of Marys'. A case in point is the *Gospel of Mary*, another non-canonical text featuring a religious leader named Mary, in which it is not fully evident whether this Mary is the Virgin or the Magdalene.

It is also possible that in some texts 'Mary' is a composite character. It has been suggested that early eastern Christian communities blended the Virgin Mary and Mary Magdalene. Although some argue this eastern combination of Marys occurred at a later date, some early evidence for a composite Mary comes from a version of the Gospel called the *Diatessaron* used in eastern churches until the 5th century. This 'Gospel' blended the four Gospels into a single narrative, and where the original text of John 20 describes Mary Magdalene meeting the resurrected Jesus, in the *Diatessaron*'s version, the Mary Jesus meets is now his mother. The same switch from the Magdalene to the Virgin also occurs in the *Questions of Bartholomew*'s account of Jesus's post-resurrection encounter (for a later image from Egypt that merges all the Gospel Marys see Figure 4).

Debating virginity in the 4th century

When Paul wrote, 'It is well for a man not to touch a woman' (1 Corinthians 7:1), the model of Christian celibacy he offered his readers was not Jesus or Mary; it was Paul himself. Among Church Fathers, it was Mary's motherhood and her maternal body that concerned them, not her virginity. With one notable exception—the *Protevangelium of James*—Mary's virginity similarly attracted little attention in apocryphal Christian texts. However, in the 4th century, a hundred years before Mary was pronounced *Aeiparthenos*, the subject of Mary's virginity took on special urgency as ascetic forms of Christianity surged in popularity. Ascetics pursued a way of life that shunned all pleasures of the body—most famously, sex—as sinful impediments to salvation. Christians had been arguing about the relative status of marriage versus sexual abstinence almost from the beginning. Nowhere, however, does the New Testament require celibacy, although Paul, who expected the world to end any minute, famously opined that celibacy was more practical. The author of 1 Timothy even denounced Christians who 'forbid marriage and demand abstinence from foods' (4:3).

Before the legalization of Christianity in 311 ended persecution, it was dying as a martyr that earned one sainthood and an assured place in heaven. Now, ascetic mortification of the flesh by purging sin and sanctifying the body offered a new type of martyrdom. This helps explain why Mary's virginity, including whether or not it was perpetual, became so important in 4th-century debates. First, as the only named virgin in the New Testament Mary became the primary biblical model for the growing number of male and female dedicated virgins. Second, as the Christian ideal of martyrs dying for their faith gave way to one of disciplining the body for one's salvation, the way Christians talked about Jesus began to shift. They began to describe Jesus, too, in ascetic terms. It was at this point that the 2nd-century *Protevangelium*, which had languished in obscurity, came to the fore. The time was ripe for both the *Protevangelium*'s ascetic agenda and its heroine, an emphatically virginal Virgin Mary. Here was an ancient (relative to the 4th century) document that highlighted the virginal purity of the mother of Jesus and in so doing guaranteed her son's freedom from sexual contamination.

At the same time, however much they idolized ascetics, the vast majority of Christians still got married and had children. Aware of this, the late 4th-century theologian Jovinian warned that the Church was in danger of creating a new and unequal hierarchy that favoured celibate Christians while at the same time excluding married Christians from leadership and community honour. For Jovinian the Virgin Mary served as the spiritual model for celibate and married Christians alike: he pointed out that Mary conceived as a virgin but then bore children with Joseph, affirming the sanctity of both virginity and marriage. Jovinian's position expressed the widespread pro-marriage position of many earlier and contemporary theologians, and it runs entirely counter to the ascetic thrust of the *Protevangelium*. The 4th century witnessed a bitter struggle between these two perspectives, and ultimately Jovinian's position, famously scorned by Jerome, was rejected. Until the Reformation in the 16th century, celibacy was ranked significantly higher than marriage, with celibate males accorded the greatest religious authority in both eastern and western Christianity.

Conclusion

At the end of the 5th century, the Virgin Mary was securely *Theotokos* and Ever-Virgin. Christians celebrated her feast days and built churches dedicated to her. Pilgrims to Jerusalem were

7. Icon of the Virgin *Theotokos* and Child Between Saints, 6th or 7th century, St Catherine's Monastery, Sinai, Egypt. Mary is portrayed as an imperial ruler on a jewelled throne; the saints flank her in the manner of high-ranking imperial court officials.

starting to visit her tomb. Most important, she interceded with her son in heaven. Mary was not yet, however, the compassionate mother familiar from later Christianity. Although there are some exceptions, both the visual and textual records lack indications that Mary was appealed to in terms of her motherly love. Images of mother and child label Mary 'Holy Mary' while the title 'Mother of God' only appears consistently on icons after the 8th century. The 7th-century *Akathistos* hymn, for example, appeals to Mary as protector rather than mother, and when Mary is depicted with Jesus positioned frontally on her lap in art of the 6th and 7th centuries she presents Christ to the world with dignity, not emotion (Figure 7). Christians of late antiquity imagined Heaven as analogous to the Byzantine court, presided over by an emperor who surrounded himself with members of the imperial family and a vast bureaucracy. Mary, her fellow saints, angels, and archangels occupied the highest circles of the heavenly court. Following the long-standing institution of political patronage, they interceded for their client-devotees. As the mother of God, Mary enjoyed the most intimate access of all.

Chapter 4
Mary the goddess?

Is the Virgin Mary a goddess? The simple answer is no. According to official Christian theology throughout the centuries, Mary is not and cannot be a goddess. Christianity is monotheistic and acknowledges only one god, even though Christians describe their god as the Holy Trinity with God the Father, God the Son, and God the Holy Ghost. An additional theological problem with calling Mary a goddess has already come up several times: Jesus's humanity came from Mary's human motherhood. If Mary were a goddess, a divine being, Jesus could not be human. The Bible never attributes divine qualities to Mary and in Luke 1:48 Mary calls herself God's humble servant.

Nevertheless, any survey devoted to the Virgin Mary must engage with the topic of Mary and goddesses for three reasons. First, there are the oft-noted parallels between the Virgin Mary and Graeco-Roman goddesses. Beliefs and rituals relating to the Virgin Mary were hardly immune to forms of cultural leakage between Christianity and the goddess-filled world in which Christianity spread. Secondly, Christian piety has often followed a separate track from official theology; over the centuries everyday Christians, theologians, and mystics, in conscious or unconscious defiance of official doctrine, have approached the Virgin as if she were a goddess, that is, as a heavenly being who wields supernatural power on her own authority. Finally, we must acknowledge forms of spirituality today, especially the New Age Goddess Movement, often centring on claims for a universal prehistoric Great Goddess with whom the Virgin Mary is frequently equated in popular culture. No credible archaeological evidence exists for any prehistoric universal mother goddess and, it should be noted, just because a culture—for example, ancient Greece or Rome—believes in a powerful goddess or goddesses does not mean human women had power, quite the opposite; but this does not negate the validity of what for many people today has effectively become a new religion: the thriving modern Goddess Movement.

Mary and goddesses in the Roman empire: similar but not equal

Christians in the Roman empire were well aware of popular mother goddesses like Egyptian Isis and Anatolia's Great Mother, Cybele. Mary as the virgin mother of the Christian god could easily call to mind not only virgin goddesses such as Athena or Artemis/Diana, who was called the 'virginal all-mother', but also Isis, who was sometimes addressed as 'the Great Virgin'. (It is a paradox of ancient religion that virgin goddesses often presided over fertility and successful childbirth.) The 5th-century women of Alexandria in Egypt addressed Mary as the 'Divine Mother', adopting an ancient title of Isis even though church authorities repeatedly discouraged attempts to call Mary *Mater Dei* (Latin, 'Mother of God') because of the title's common association with Graeco-Roman goddesses. *Theotokos* may also have been a title of Isis as mother of the god Horus. Long after the Council of Ephesus, Rome's continued hesitation to acknowledge Mary publicly as *Theotokos* indicates the western Church's misgivings around the title's links with goddess worship.

In early Christianity one person's saint could be another person's divinity. When popular enthusiasm for martyrs and saints gained ground in the 4th and 5th centuries, some influential bishops resisted, complaining that the growing cult of saints amounted to worshipping dead people as if they were divine. Syrian Bishop Theodoret of Cyrrhus (*Therapeutikê* 8.15–30) freely acknowledged that Christian saints and martyrs resembled the many Graeco-Roman divinized heroes such as Herakles/Hercules, but clarified that the old gods were actually demons and immoral and therefore invalid. Saints' shrines sometimes took over hero shrines, offering Christian worshippers the same types of healing and guidance provided earlier by the divinized hero. Once Mary was included in the exalted ranks of saints and martyrs, it was almost inevitable that her role as the mother of the Christian God would suggest to many former followers of Graeco-Roman deities that, like mother goddesses, Mary could influence human and earthly fertility.

An example of Mary's overlap in function with goddesses of fertility appears in Palestinian Dormition texts from the 5th century which attest to three commemorations of the Virgin over the Palestinian agricultural year. Mary is specifically called upon to bless seeds in winter, protect crops from pests and destructive weather during the growing season, and then to ensure a rich harvest. No single explanation or single goddess cult accounts for the process by which Mary acquired some attributes of Mediterranean goddesses. Ancient devotion to goddesses of fertility, war, death, or other phenomena always developed locally, and similarities between goddesses across time and space exist for a variety of reasons including universal human concerns and cultural interactions based on conquest or appropriation.

The Church in the east tended to worry less than the west about applying goddess language to the Virgin. For example, Constantine dedicated his new capital Constantinople to the goddess *Nea Roma* ('New Rome'), who often took the form of Athena carrying a spear and distaff, symbols of her two domains: war and weaving. As guardian of Constantinople, Athena appeared on Byzantine coins as late as the mid-6th century, so for a while Athena and Mary essentially coexisted. Perhaps not surprisingly, then, in 626 after Constantinople's escape from siege by the Avars, its citizens credited the *Theotokos* with a display of martial prowess in language previously used for Athena. George of Pisidia's poem, *Bellum avaricum* ('Avar War'), depicts the 'Invincible Virgin' in full cry:

> ...arbiter and general of battle...she who gave birth without seed bent the arrows, opposed the shields, mingled invisibly among the adversaries, flinging arrows, inflicting losses, blunting the blows of the sword, upsetting and sinking the ships and all the invaders to the bottom of the sea...The Virgin fought in the frontline...[she] did not hesitate to intervene herself in combat.

The poet even applies Athena's traditional Greek titles *Parthenos* ('Virgin') and *Promachos* ('First in the Line of Battle') to Mary. Mary's resemblance to Athena extended even to Athena's patronage of spinning and weaving. Images of the *Protevangelium*'s Annunciation scene where Gabriel comes upon Mary as she spins thread for the Temple curtain became so popular that Mary was closely associated with weaving, not just in art but in theological discourse. While Mary took on characteristics of Athena and other goddesses, however, it was always within the unique context of her own role as the mother of Jesus.

Equally important for understanding Christian–pagan interactions and Mary's place within them were the many different regional female deities and spirits whose functions could overlap, be absorbed, or be transformed in light of local Christian practice. While sometimes consciously in competition with older religious traditions, local Christianities interacted with local traditions. Under the radar, as it were, of ecclesiastical control, newly self-identifying Christians maintained or adapted older domestic and civic devotional habits. It can be difficult, for example, to determine from the text of a magical amulet whether its owner was Jewish, Christian, pagan, or some combination thereof. A 7th-century Egyptian healing spell refers to, 'Jesus Horus the son of Isis' rather than son of Mary. Versions of another spell, the 'Prayer of Mary Dissolving Chains' (see Figure 4, Chapter 3), is still used by Egyptian Copts today. Its language has parallels with popular ancient spells calling upon Isis, the mistress of magical forces who releases one from troubles, as when Mary commands,

> Let all things submit to me for I am Mary, I am Mariham, I am the mother of the life of the whole world... let the rock split before me today, let the iron dissolve before me today, let the demons withdraw before me... let the doors that are bolted and closed open for me at once.

Because the familiar images of Mary nursing Jesus at her breast resemble depictions of Isis nursing her son Horus, it has been claimed, albeit erroneously, that Mary was 'just Isis with a different name', or that Isis imagery was simply transferred to Mary. In the early Christian period, however, images of Isis nursing Horus were far outnumbered by other types of Isis imagery and various other goddesses were depicted suckling a divine son—never a daughter—on coins and other media. Images of Mary with Jesus at her breast took centuries to evolve from the Virgin and child motif that itself originated in the Adoration of the Magi (see Figure 3, Chapter 3). Somewhat surprisingly God, more often than Mary, was described by early church leaders as a tender nursing mother. Using the same gender-fluid metaphorical approach we saw in the *Odes of Solomon*, Augustine taught in the late 4th century that

> for those who become children before God, he becomes father and mother to them: a father because he builds, summons, judges, rules: a mother because he caresses, nourishes, feeds with milk and gathers together.

Images of *Maria lactans* (Latin, 'Mary nursing') began to appear in Byzantine art of the 6th century, but only became widespread during the Middle Ages and Renaissance. In the 6th century, clearly identifiable *Maria lactans* figures appeared on the cell walls of Egyptian monks. In Graeco-Roman culture where wet nurses were the norm, the primary connotation of suckling a child was not always motherly intimacy; within their religious contexts, the milk of Isis and of Mary served different purposes: where Isis's milk endowed Horus (embodied in the human Pharaoh) with divinity and kingship, Mary's milk signified Jesus's humanity.

One likely inspiration for early Christian depictions of Mary suckling Jesus is Roman imperial propaganda. Roman coins show the empress or a goddess standing or seated on a throne with one or even two children at her breast. On one spectacular gold coin Constantine's empress, Fausta, nurses a child while military guards flank her throne on the right and left. This royal theme predominates on 6th-century icons and jewellery where Mary holds Jesus and sits like an empress on an elaborate jewelled throne flanked by an honour guard of saints and angels (see Figure 7, Chapter 3).

Mary and the goddess question in medieval and early modern Christianity

Catholic and Orthodox doctrine alike has always stipulated that 'worship' is appropriate only for a deity and thus is owed to God alone. 'Veneration' is offered to saints and to the Virgin Mary, although the eminent 13th-century Catholic theologian Thomas Aquinas added that Mary merited super-veneration. Official Orthodox and Catholic theology is adamant that only by interceding with Christ are Mary and her fellow saints able to channel divine power. (Most Protestants, remember, do not recognize intercession.) Technically speaking, then, Christians cannot 'worship' Mary.

On the other hand, in their enthusiasm for Mary some theologians and mystics over the centuries could be said to have blurred the division between veneration and worship. This has especially been true in the west where devotion to the Virgin expanded rapidly during the Middle Ages and persisted in the Catholic Church after the Reformation. Richard of Saint-Laurent (13th century) claimed that by carrying Jesus in her womb, 'Mary was not only made the hostess or guest-house of the Son of God, but rather of the whole Trinity'. This phrasing inflated the traditional understanding, that only Christ dwelt in Mary's womb, to the entire Trinity, thereby suggesting Mary encompasses and outranks the Trinity. Saint-Laurent's words were visualized in a type of medieval statuette called a 'shrine Madonna' which consisted of a figure of Mary that swings open to reveal tiny figures of the Trinity (i.e. Father, Son, Holy Spirit) hidden inside her body. (Shrine Madonnas were later prohibited by the Pope.)

A late 16th-century example of Mary as divine comes from the Franciscan Lawrence of Brindisi in Sermon 5 of his *Mariale*:

> God has set Mary over the works of His hands. She is the Goddess of Heaven, the Queen of the universe, the true Spouse of the omnipotent God, the true Mother of the almighty Christ. She stands at the right hand of God as heaven's exalted Queen.

The Franciscans, traditionally Marian maximalists, campaigned in the Middle Ages to recognize Mary as 'Co-Redemptrix' (Co-Redeemer), a title which, in essence, elevated Mary to divine status equal to Jesus. The movement receded in the post-Reformation era precisely because the Council of Trent in the 16th century refused to claim for Mary an equal role with Jesus in human salvation.

Today, some conservative Catholic groups still lobby for Mary's Co-Redemptrix status, but have faced consistent Vatican resistance, famously expressed by Pope John XXIII when he pronounced, 'The Madonna is not pleased when she is put above her son.' In any event, claims for Co-Redemptrix and images like Shrine Madonnas helped fuel the often oversimplified accusations by 16th-century Reformers that, as they put it, 'godless Papists' had turned Mary into a goddess.

Mary, God's ancient consort, and wisdom

Thus far we have considered the question of Mary and goddess status in the context of Christian monotheism. However, Christianity's roots go back to biblical Israel, which scholars have demonstrated was not always monotheistic. A series of remarkable archaeological discoveries in the 1970s revealed that the ancient Israelites had worshipped not just God but also a fertility goddess, possibly named Asherah and sometimes called the queen of heaven. Up to at least the 6th century BCE, this goddess, one of whose primary symbols was a tree of life, was understood to be God's wife and lover.

As Israel grew increasingly monotheistic, memories of this goddess were suppressed, but she was not fully erased. The Bible contains clues that Israel's former goddess survived in the form of a new abstract concept, God's wisdom, personified as a woman. The biblical books of Proverbs and Job and the apocryphal book of Wisdom (sometimes called the Wisdom of Solomon) contain passages devoted to the female-gendered Wisdom of God—the Woman, Wisdom—who, according to Wisdom 8:3, 'glorifies her noble birth by living with God, and the Lord of all loves her'.

More than a thousand years later, the Catholic Church after the Council of Trent equated the Virgin Mary and God's Wisdom by introducing biblical Wisdom texts into the official liturgy for the Feast of Mary's Immaculate Conception. All unwittingly, then, the Tridentine liturgists who diligently resisted attempts to elevate

Mary to full divine status chose scriptures for Marian feasts which link her to Israel's ancient goddess. The Immaculate Conception of Mary, unlike the Annunciation or Jesus's Nativity, had no clear biblical basis. Bible verses about Woman Wisdom supplied a rich, if metaphorical, vein of biblical precedent. Just as typological interpretation turned female biblical heroes like Sarah or Esther into foreshadowings or 'types' of Mary, the biblical description of Wisdom as a woman provided the Catholic Church with a biblical typology for Mary's Immaculate Conception. Woman Wisdom's description of herself in Proverbs 8:22 and 8:30, when read through a Marian lens, suggested that as God's Wisdom, Mary existed in a timeless dimension long before her actual conception:

> When [God] established the heavens, I was there…
> when He marked out the foundations of the earth,
> then I was beside Him, like a master worker.

Catholic artists were instructed to depict Mary the Immaculate Conception (i.e. the person who was conceived immaculately, without sin) as a young girl hovering in the heavens. These verses remained in the liturgy until the Vatican II reforms of the 1960s.

By equating the biblical Woman Wisdom with Mary in the liturgy, the Council of Trent was carrying on a Marian theme which had been envisioned earlier in a popular type of medieval Madonna and Child statue called a 'Throne of Wisdom' (Latin, *Sedes Sapientiae*). This is a distinct group of small European 12th-century Mary sculptures, mostly carved from wood. The celebrated Spanish Black Virgin of Montserrat (Figure 8) is a classic example. Thirty-eight inches (96.5 cm) tall, she sits squarely on a throne with Jesus as a little king seated on her lap. Throne of Wisdom statues were viewed frontally so that Jesus appeared completely framed by Mary's body, an allusion to Mary's all-enclosing womb.

8. Black Madonna, Montserrat, Spain; wood; 12th century; Throne of Wisdom sculpture.

In the New Testament and early Christianity it had been Jesus, not Mary, who was identified with the Old Testament figure of Wisdom, despite Wisdom's feminine gender. Thus the phrase 'Throne of Wisdom' principally means 'a throne for Wisdom—Jesus—to sit on'; it is Jesus's throne. But grammatical ambiguity allows another interpretation; just as 'throne of wood' means a throne made out of wood, 'Throne of Wisdom' can also mean a throne *made* of Wisdom. In this case Mary, the throne, is divine Wisdom, just as Tridentine liturgy asserted.

Mary and Aztec goddesses

The Council of Trent promoted uniform Christ-centric doctrine and sought to subdue practices, many of them related to Mary, that the council deemed superstitious and undoctrinal. While the council was meeting in Italy, however, European missionaries in the New World capitalized on similarities between the Virgin Mary and local goddesses in their campaigns to convert indigenous peoples to Catholicism. In 16th-century colonial Mexico, the Virgin of Guadalupe became a genuinely transcultural Virgin Mary with links to pre-colonial Aztec goddesses. Mexico's most celebrated Virgin, Our Lady of Guadalupe (Figure 9) represents an instance when the Church strategically accommodated a goddess tradition and was in turn transformed by the encounter. The Virgin's reported appearances in December 1531 to a recent Aztec convert rank among the most renowned of her many earthly encounters. All doubts in Bishop Zumárraga's mind that the Virgin could have spoken with Juan Diego (Cuauhtlatoatzin, 'Talking Eagle' in Nahuatl) fell away when unseasonal roses spilled miraculously from Juan Diego's cactus-fibre *tilma* (cloak) and a life-sized image of the Virgin appeared on its surface.

According to the traditional story, Juan Diego's meetings with the Virgin took place on the hill of Tepeyac, north of Mexico City. The

9. Our Lady of Guadalupe, Anonymous, 16th century. Basilica of Our Lady of Guadalupe, Mexico City.

hill had been the site of a pre-colonial pilgrimage shrine dedicated to a group of earth goddesses collectively called *Tonantzin* or 'Our Revered Mother'. Mary, speaking perfect Nahuatl, asked that a shrine in her honour be built on Tepeyac hill. The image of the Virgin on Juan Diego's *tilma* closely resembles European Virgins of the Immaculate Conception, but it has other details considered to be Indian: Mary's brown skin and black hair, a cloak the aquamarine colour of royal Aztec quetzal-feather capes, and an Aztec pregnancy belt. In the ensuing centuries, despite misgivings, the Church did not deny Tepeyac's prior status as a goddess shrine. Today some 20 million pilgrims a year, more than to any other Christian shrine, visit the Basilica of Guadalupe at Tepeyac to gaze upon Juan Diego's *tilma* with its image of *La Morenita* ('Little Brown One').

Mary, popular spirituality, and goddesses

In contemporary European and American popular spirituality, goddesses from many times and places are routinely identified with each other and with the Virgin Mary. On the internet, a useful gauge of popular spirituality, Mary may be identified as the 'Christian Goddess of Compassion', to cite a randomly accessed site, as well as the 'Christian avatar' of a universal goddess, and the equivalent of the Tibetan Tara, Japanese Kwan-yin, Egyptian Isis, and Hindu Lakshmi. Across the internet and in popular culture, enthusiasm for indiscriminately lumping goddesses together is traceable to mid-20th-century feminism, heightened concerns about the environment, and appreciation for indigenous and eastern spirituality stimulated by civil rights and ethnic identity movements. Popular websites and books tend to describe goddesses, often including Mary, using gender stereotypes of feminine power expressed in terms of nurture, compassion, and the natural world.

This is a well-intentioned, if limiting, frame of reference and is often associated with psychologist Carl Jung. Praising Pope Pius XII's declaration of the doctrine of the Assumption of the Virgin in 1950, Jung—not himself a Catholic—maintained that at last the Catholic Church was embracing 'the feminine element, of the earth, the body, and matter in general', divine qualities that Jung believed had been excluded by the Church's 'masculine doctrine of the Trinity'. While at various times Mary has certainly been associated with these qualities, a full picture of her encompasses much more, and to assume they constitute the essence of women's or Mary's nature is to perpetuate stereotypes that are often culturally imposed. On the other hand, one need not equate compassion, tenderness, and the powers of the natural world solely with the feminine to recognize that humans have a natural yearning for divine tenderness and compassion and to encounter the divine in the natural world. Once Mary's loving, motherly side began to be emphasized (around the 10th century), it has often been through Mary that Christians sought and found divine compassion.

The Black Madonna

At the intersection of popular contemporary goddess spirituality and devotion to the Virgin are the so-called Black Madonnas. At issue here is a group of images of Madonna and Child from the Middle Ages mostly located in historically white Catholic European countries, especially France, Germany, Spain, and Italy. These are a different category from modern images of black-skinned Madonnas in Africa or the United States whose worshippers share her dark coloration. As for Orthodox icons, Mary's coloration may often look somewhat dark, but the Black Madonna is not a significant feature of Orthodox Christianity. Since the 1950s, these medieval Black Madonnas have often been explained uncritically in terms of pre-Christian European earth or mother goddesses or the 'divine feminine'.

Unfortunately, no coherent set of criteria has ever been developed for defining a Black Madonna. Colouring can run from light brown to inky black, and paint samples from Black Madonnas have revealed that many images were not even originally dark. A scientific analysis of Black Madonnas in Spain found a great deal of colour manipulation over the centuries, with images regularly changing colour. The Black Virgin of Montserrat even has blonde hair (see Figure 8). The Mexican Virgin of Guadalupe, whose skin is sometimes described as ashen, often appears in lists of Black Madonnas; at Our Lady of Guadalupe's great basilica outside Mexico City, the stained-glass version of Our Lady has much darker skin than the Virgin on Juan Diego's *tilma*.

The form of the Black Madonna varies, but most were created between the 13th and 15th centuries. A few are two-dimensional Byzantine-style icons like Poland's Black Madonna of Czestochowa, but many are seated Throne of Wisdom statues or, especially in southern Germany, Switzerland, and northern Italy, Mary may stand with Jesus on her arm. Black Madonna shrines attracted the greatest number of pilgrims between 1550 and 1900 and were often the primary national Madonna, as was the case with the Virgins of Montserrat, du Puy in France, Einsiedeln in Switzerland, and Loreto in Italy.

Enthusiasts often point out that Black Madonna shrines are situated on sites of pre-Christian goddess worship to claim that the Black Madonna is a Christianized goddess or the survival of an earth-centred pre-Christian spirituality. This is true of many Black Madonna shrines, but this is hardly unique to Black Madonnas; even more churches of 'white' Madonnas belong to this category, and countless churches dedicated to Christ or the saints were also built on pre-Christian sacred sites. The supposedly unique powers of Black Madonnas are attributed equally to other miraculous Madonnas.

Until very recently, studies of Black Madonnas have failed to take into consideration the ways cultural values and ideas of blackness have shifted over time. The fact that, in the Graeco-Roman world, statues of the mother goddesses Isis, Cybele, and Diana could be carved from black or dark stone does not mean, for example, that Black Madonnas are related to Isis; in the ancient world, it was the shininess of black stone that signified divinity. Whether a Madonna is black and what her blackness means are a matter of cultural perception, and that perception depends fundamentally on historical context. This includes the changing ways in which devotion to Madonnas celebrated as 'black' was promoted by the Catholic Church. The reason Black Madonnas today are so often labelled 'enigmatic' or 'mysterious' is because today blackness tends to be conceived of in terms of race. In earlier centuries the Virgin's blackness had different connotations.

The Church's initial focus on the Virgin's blackness coincided with efforts after the Council of Trent to revive medieval pilgrimage sites and promote devotion to miraculous images in deliberate opposition to Protestant rejection of religious imagery. In the 17th century the Church sought out and then published legends about the origins of the miraculous Black Madonnas. The stories invariably told of the miraculous discovery of the image, usually in a rustic natural setting like a cave, a tree trunk, or riverbank. The discovery legends stressed, however, that the newly found image originally came from the Holy Land but had been hidden long ago to protect it. Furthermore, it was often claimed that the image was created in the Holy Land by St Luke himself while the Virgin modelled for him. This fitted nicely with the exotic (to Catholics) dusky-hued Byzantine icon Madonnas they occasionally encountered, while the dark wood of the Throne of Wisdom statues suggested precious foreign woods like ebony and cedar that were associated with the Holy Land. Blackness here signified miraculous power derived from a threefold combination of wonders: the image's antiquity dating back to Jesus's lifetime; its origin in Mary's own homeland; and the confidence guaranteed by its attribution to St Luke that the image preserved the Virgin's authentic likeness.

While legends recounted popular stories about the statues, the Church also offered a biblical precedent for the Black Madonna in a verse from the Song of Songs. In the Latin Vulgate, the official Bible of the Catholic Church, Song of Songs 1:5 reads, 'I am black, but beautiful'. (The Hebrew actually says, 'I am black *and* beautiful.') Because church leaders had for centuries equated the woman of the Song of Songs with the Virgin Mary, this verse provided a scriptural link between Mary and the blackness of the Black Madonna statues. It was additionally explained that Mary's blackness came from her sorrow at the Crucifixion or indicated her humility.

Surprisingly, before the 18th century in Germany and Italy writers who described the Madonnas of Einsiedeln and Loreto never mention the statues' unusual colouring, nor is the dark colouring indicated in contemporary illustrations where she appears clearly as white. Before 1700, when individual pilgrims donated amateur paintings to the Einsiedeln Virgin illustrating miracles she had accomplished for them, they depicted the Virgin as white, usually with golden hair. This is not because these Virgins were not yet 'black', but because the image's colour, however it had come about, was not read by devotees in racial terms. Even today, Italy's Black Virgin of Loreto is white and blonde-haired in the paintings and frescos that decorate the church dedicated to Mary of Loreto in Rome.

In the 19th century several factors converged to diminish and then erase the prestige that had been accorded Black Madonnas on the basis of their supposed antiquity and authenticity. One was the new pseudo-science of race, informed by centuries of European participation in the enslavement of black Africans. Hierarchical arrangements of human groups, with whites at the top and blacks at the bottom, were received as irrefutable science. For the first time, Mary's blackness struck people as enigmatic, even problematic, and for the first time, the Catholic Church referred to the Madonnas' blackness as the natural effect of age or the inevitable accumulation of smoke from candles, lamps, and incense.

Simultaneously, the authenticity factor enjoyed by the Black Madonnas as original creations of St Luke from Mary's lifetime was eclipsed by reports of personal interactions with Mary by 19th-century visionaries like Catherine Labouré of the *Miraculous Medal*, discussed in Chapter 1 (Figure 1), and Bernadette of Lourdes. In contemporary illustrations, Mary appears to the visionaries as a white woman. The Madonna in these apparitions was often closely associated with the doctrine of the Immaculate Conception and its semi-official colour, white for purity. Nineteenth-century art historians' consensus that white marble Greek and Roman sculptures were the ideal of human beauty further encouraged the perception of whiteness as aesthetically superior. Today the two most common explanations for the Black Madonnas are either that they have darkened with age or that their darkness relates to a supposed ancient goddess; as we have seen, however, the historical record points to a more complicated set of answers that relate to changing modes of Marian devotion over time.

Conclusion

Through the centuries the Virgin has been, as historian E. Ann Matter wrote in an important essay, part of the 'continuum of the Christian conception of divinity', and as such, Mary has been 'a crucial part of the Christian understanding of God'. Ordinary Christians have seldom troubled themselves with historical context or theological complexities. They have praised and petitioned the Virgin in the assurance that their Mother in heaven would hear and respond. From an anthropological rather than theological perspective, how an entity functions determines divine status regardless of official doctrine. If Christians pray to a being in heaven such as Mary and believe Mary possesses her own miracle-working powers that bring tangible blessings, then functionally, Mary is a goddess.

Chapter 5
Eastern Mary—Byzantium and Islam

To Orthodox Christians the *Akathistos* hymn to the *Theotokos* is unrivalled in beauty. It goes in part,

> While singing to Thine Offspring [Jesus], we all praise Thee as a living temple, O *Theotokos*;
>
> for the Lord who holds all things in His hand dwelt in Thy womb,
>
> and He sanctified and glorified Thee, and taught all to cry to Thee:
>
> …Rejoice, O Bride Unwedded!

The hymn (late 5th or early 6th century) was traditionally credited to Romanos Melodos, the most illustrious of Byzantine poets, though scholars now doubt the attribution. Its Greek title means 'not sitting' to indicate it must be sung while standing reverently. This chapter will consider Marian ideals in Byzantine Christianity as well as the Islamic view of Maryam which at once reflects and rejects the Byzantine worldview from which Islam, in part, emerged.

Byzantine Virgin: the historical context

The Roman empire became the Byzantine empire when the Emperor Constantine and his fellow tetrarchs legalized Christianity in 311, although the empire only became officially

Christian in 380, the year Emperor Theodosian made Christianity the imperial religion. When Constantine seized power, the Roman empire was already divided administratively into eastern and western parts. Under Constantine, Rome remained the western capital, but in 330 Constantine established a new eastern capital city at the ancient city of Byzantium, which he renamed Constantinople. The original city name is the source of the term, 'Byzantine'.

In 476, when the western half of the empire broke up under pressure from Christian barbarians, the eastern half of the Roman empire survived as the Byzantine empire. The fall of the western empire, however, did not prevent church authorities in both the west and east from continuing to consult closely. Only in 1054 did doctrinal differences set in motion the Great Schism which ultimately split the Church into the Catholic west and Orthodox east. By then, the two regions had grown apart, differing not only in theology but also, crucially, in language, with eastern Christians speaking and worshipping in Greek, Coptic, and Syriac, while Latin predominated in the west.

It was in the east that Christians celebrated the first Marian festivals, dedicated the earliest Marian churches, and depicted Mary on coins. As new feast days in honour of Mary were proclaimed in Constantinople, Rome and the west followed suit. The first Marian relics were also discovered and venerated in the east. Relics of the Virgin were first promoted and celebrated in Constantinople in the later 5th century, only 150 years after the capital's founding. Even before the Virgin was given credit for delivering Constantinople from Avar–Persian attack in the 7th century, the capital city was already a veritable *Theotokoupolis* or *Theotokos*-City.

For considerable portions of the 8th and 9th centuries, Byzantium was rocked internally by a movement known as Iconoclasm that condemned and destroyed most religious images. As a result, the few examples of early Byzantine art that survived can only be found in places beyond the reach of the iconoclasts, most notably Rome and Ravenna, Italy. In the later 9th century when religious images were again permitted, Byzantine Christians began to treat painted icons of the Virgin like relics, with the same miracle-working powers.

Muslim expansion in the later 7th century seriously threatened the Byzantine empire, but the empire survived and even revived. In all, Byzantium endured for over 1,000 years, only falling to the Muslim Ottoman Turks in 1453. The Orthodox faith survived 1453 and today the majority of Orthodox Christians live in eastern Europe, Russia, Greece, and Cyprus, with threatened populations in the Middle East, a vibrant presence in Ethiopia, and a large diaspora worldwide. Marian veneration was central in Byzantine picty and political culture, and the areas that Byzantium lost to Islam—Egypt, Syria-Palestine, and Mesopotamia—had been home to some of the most vibrant Marian traditions of all. Since Muslims revere Jesus as a prophet, it should come as no surprise that his mother features prominently in the Qur'an and that Maryam is one of the most revered women in the Muslim tradition.

Proclus' first homily and an icon: a Mary primer

Byzantine theologians, preachers, and poets competed to praise the *Theotokos*, deploying an array of Old Testament references to celebrate her role in God's plan of salvation as well as her active defence of the empire. The most influential homily on the Mother of God in the history of Christianity was preached in Constantinople for the Virgin's festival of 429 by Proclus, a bishop in the Empress Pulcheria's circle. The eloquence with which Proclus' homily justified Mary's claim to be *Theotokos* thrilled the crowd and directly affected the outcome of the Council of Ephesus in 431.

The homily's influence rests not so much in its unimpeachable orthodox Christology but in the compelling Marian imagery

Proclus assembled to advance that Christology. In fact, Proclus provides a basic primer of Marian metaphors that were endlessly repeated in writing and art. A resplendent 12th-century icon of the Annunciation translated Proclus' themes into images; by examining the details of the icon we can appreciate more fully the symbolic language of the homily (Figure 10a). We should keep in mind that icons are more than religious pictures painted on wooden panels; for the Orthodox, icons are windows offering humans direct access to the divine.

The Annunciation icon was probably created by a monk of St Catherine's Monastery at the foot of Mt Sinai. It depicts the two figures essential to all Annunciation scenes; the Angel Gabriel, golden robes aflutter, approaches the Virgin. She sits on a throne-like chair and tilts her head toward her sudden visitor. Mary's house appears behind her, with other houses of Nazareth in the distance. Typically for icons, the background gleams with gold leaf. Gold, which cannot tarnish, symbolizes the eternal divine light of heaven and always surrounds holy figures. Along the bottom a stream teems with birds and fish; at the top, from a golden half-circle—the light of God—a dove descends in a shaft of light. This description, however, fails to convey the dense theological work going on in the icon, and here is where Proclus' homily comes in.

Mindful of the theological dispute that had precipitated the upcoming Council of Ephesus, Proclus needed to explain to ordinary people in his audience why, to bring about the mysterious union of Jesus's two natures, Mary *had* to be *Theotokos*. Without Mary's virginal motherhood, God could not have become human, suffered death on the cross, and thereby, said Proclus, 'buy us out of slavery...to the devil'. The Annunciation icon signals Mary's humanity by the dark royal reds and purples of her clothing and cushion, contrasting sharply with the overall divine light of gleaming gold.

Proclus began with Mary as the second Eve, 'the spiritual paradise of the second Adam'. An Orthodox viewer would see the icon's allusion to Paradise and the Second Eve in the Edenic abundance of life along the stream at Mary's feet. Such fertility also evokes the springtime season of the Feast of the Annunciation. The walled garden full of trees and birds on the roof of Mary's house also recalls Eden or Paradise (Figure 10b) as well as another Bible verse already interpreted as referring to Mary: 'A garden locked is my sister, my bride' (Song of Songs 4:12). The locked (or walled) garden refers to Mary's virginity and to her womb, the new Garden of Eden, where the New Adam, Jesus, dwells.

Proclus praises Mary, the New Eve, as the personification of her own pregnant womb, the 'spiritual paradise' where the New Adam took on flesh. In Proclus' unexpected imagery, Mary's womb is 'the workshop of the union of natures; the marketplace of the contract of salvation:' a 'marketplace' for conceiving the child who will 'buy us out of slavery' and a 'workshop' where the flesh of the saviour is woven. The icon pictures the 'union of natures' in progress before our eyes, despite centuries of deterioration; a faint image of the infant Jesus (Figure 10b) is still visible on Mary's chest, a prototype of the transparent womb of Damien Hirst's *The Virgin Mother*.

Proclus also uses well-known Marian symbolism in the burning bush of Exodus 3. As Gregory of Nyssa wrote in his *Life of Moses*, 'The light of divinity...did not consume the burning bush, even as the flower of [Mary's] virginity was not withered by giving birth.' Proclus' ensuing phrase, 'virgin and heaven, the only bridge from God to mankind', elevates Mary above human nature—albeit metaphorically. For Proclus, Mary's womb emphatically belongs to a human mother, but in his heightened poetic diction, Mary skirts the edges of the divine, precisely the effect of the icon's golden light that gleams all around the Virgin, not to mention Mary's jewelled golden throne and footstool so evocative of emperors, empresses, and Jesus in majesty. Even if only figuratively, the

10a. Icon: Annunciation, 12th century, wood; Monastery of
St Catherine, Sinai, Egypt.

10b. Detail of Figure 10a, Jesus in Mary's womb, curtain at entrance to Mary's room, roof garden.

Virgin has been elevated to 'heaven', making it easier to imagine Mary as *Theotokos*, the 'one who gives birth to God'.

Finally, Proclus links the gestation of God in Mary's womb to the act of weaving, the female activity that symbolized chastity. Weaving was also associated with Eve, to whom, according to Epiphanius of Salamis, God gave the 'wisdom of weaving', a skill humans needed to cover the shame of nakedness for which Eve was blamed. Christians were long accustomed to applying the symbolism of clothing to salvation, teaching that with the fall, Adam lost the robe of glory he wore in Paradise. In a gracious exchange, Jesus the New Adam clothed himself in the old Adam's fallen flesh so that, by baptism, Christians might once again put on robes of glory. Mary's womb, declared Proclus, was the 'awesome loom of the divine economy upon which the robe of union was ineffably woven'.

'Robe of union' refers to Jesus's two natures. Preachers and painters linked the theme of Mary weaving the flesh of Jesus in her womb and the *Protevangelium*'s account the of Annunciation to Mary as she was spinning thread for the Temple, the scene on our icon. From the ball of yarn in Mary's lap a thread extends up to the bunch of yarn in her left hand. A blood-red thread passes directly over the ghostly figure of Christ, suggesting nothing so much as an umbilical cord and simultaneously a thread pulled by a shuttle through a loom.

The ball of yarn with its strategically placed red thread alludes to yet another influential textile-based Marian metaphor, one that equated Jesus's flesh with the Jerusalem Temple curtain, the very curtain on which the Annunciate Mary was working. The New Testament book of Hebrews referred to the '...new and living way that [Jesus] opened for us through the [Temple] curtain, that is, through his flesh' (Hebrews 10:20). Mary's womb, then, resembles both Paradise, where God dwells, and the Jerusalem Temple where God's presence filled the space screened off by the Temple curtain, known as the Holy of Holies. The Annunciation icon alludes explicitly to this theme of the Temple and its significance in Christian salvation: at the entrance to Mary's bedroom, a curtain has been pulled aside, symbolizing Jesus as the Temple curtain and simultaneously pointing ahead to the moment of Jesus's death on the cross when Matthew, Mark, and Luke report that the Temple curtain split in two. The torn Temple curtain mirrored the purpose of Jesus's death: the barrier of sin no longer kept humans from God.

How did Mary conceive?

The Annunciation icon, like Proclus' Homily, takes for granted one answer to a nagging question: how did Mary become pregnant? Early Christian writers variously attributed the miraculous conception to one or another of the human senses, in each case trying to reconcile the bodily reality of Mary's pregnancy with minimal bodily involvement. They suggested that Mary was 'perfumed' pregnant through her sense of smell, or that she swallowed a cloud of divine light, or she conceived through her eyes by seeing a baby boy in a vision. Proclus, however, voices the emerging consensus: Mary conceived by 'the Word, who entered in [to her womb] through her sense of hearing'.

On the icon, as Mary turns toward Gabriel, she tilts her head ever so slightly and lifts her right ear. The notion of conception through the ear originated in the Gospel of John's identification of Jesus as the Word of God made flesh. When Mary listened to Gabriel's words, Jesus the Word of God became flesh in Mary's womb. Furthermore, just as the concept of Mary spinning thread could be connected to Eve, conception by ear linked Mary and Eve because of the earth-shaking consequences after each woman listened to the 'word' of a stranger.

Despite its early popularity, aural conception was eventually superseded, although the idea lingered in Syria and Egypt, and eastern and western artists occasionally illustrated it. W. B. Yeats's poem 'Mother of God' (1933) repeats the theme as Mary describes her feelings at the Annunciation:

> The threefold terror of love; a fallen flare
> Through the hollow of an ear;
> Wings beating about the room;
> The terror of all terrors that I bore
> The Heavens in my womb.

Worried that sound's invisibility undermined the crucial flesh-and-blood reality of Mary's pregnancy, theologians turned to another explanation by fixing on light and glass. A beam of light, unlike sound, could be perceived by the human eye, while glass was transparent yet solid to the touch. A sermon by Pseudo-Athanasius uses both concepts:

> Just as sunlight passes through a pane of glass without shattering it, so too did the Son of God pass through the glass windows, that is through the ears of the Virgin, without destroying her virginity.

Light imagery derived from Jesus's pronouncement, 'I am the Light of the world' (John 8:12), and from earliest Christianity, Jesus had been associated with light. The metaphor of light passing through glass gave theologians and artists yet another reason to characterize Mary in terms of divine light, exactly as the vast stretches of gold on the Annunciation icon overwhelm the viewer with their luminosity. (When a Renaissance artist includes a glass window in an Annunciation scene, we are witnessing the unimpeded passage of light through glass and an allusion to Mary's virginal conception of Jesus.)

Relics

A major feature of Byzantine Christianity was the cult of relics. A relic consists of the bodily remains of a saint or martyr or is an object that has come into physical contact with holy remains. Constantine was said to have imported relics to secure the safety of Constantinople just as Rome claimed its martyr tombs protected the city like an impregnable wall. A non-Christian might look at a relic and see rubbish, but to the eyes of faith each relic was precious, connected by an invisible link to the saint in heaven and the saint's intercessory powers. Christian pilgrims not only travelled to sacred places like the Holy Land with its links to Jesus, but also visited illustrious relics at shrines near and far. In turn, relics carried back by pilgrims from the remote Holy Land erased geographical distance to guarantee the worshipper access to the same power that saturated Christianity's most sacred topography.

Mary and Jesus differed from saints and martyrs in leaving no body on earth. Christendom's most precious relic was not, therefore, a bit of body, but the wood of the True Cross on which Jesus died and which tradition claimed Constantine's mother, Helena, had discovered in Jerusalem. Jerusalem was also the source for the Marian relics that began to arrive in Constantinople during the 5th century. By the 12th century, visitors to the city could report encountering not just the Virgin's milk but her spindle and Jesus's swaddling clothes. Most powerful of all Constantinople's miracle-working relics and the emotional centre of early Byzantine Marian devotion was a garment worn by the Virgin. Theodore of Synkellos in the 7th century claimed, 'we believe that it not only clothed the Mother of God but that in it she actually wrapped the Word of God himself when he was a little child and gave him milk'. Contradictory accounts obscure the actual type of garment it was; sometimes it is called a veil, at other times a shroud, sometimes a belt (or girdle, a wide cloth worn as a belt). Whatever it was (let's call it Mary's mantle), it was the first and most enduringly famous of the miracle-working relics of the Virgin.

Mary's mantle was housed in the Blachernai church, the first, the most important, and eventually the largest *Theotokos* church in

Constantinople. Tradition credited its construction to Pulcheria, imperial champion of the *Theotokos*, although historians think it was built by a slightly later empress. Nevertheless, according to one of the relic's origin legends, Pulcheria asked Bishop Juvenal of Jerusalem for relics of the Virgin for her new church at Blachernai. Juvenal recounted the story of Mary's Dormition to explain to Pulcheria why no bodily relics of Mary existed. Juvenal explained that the Dormition story was not scriptural but that it merited reverence nevertheless, and he offered an alternative set of relics: a late-arriving apostle had inspected Mary's coffin and although her corpse had vanished, some clothes were left behind. Juvenal reportedly sent a 'holy casket carefully sealed up with the dresses of the All-Holy *Theotokos* Mary inside', which Pulcheria faithfully deposited in the Blachernai.

Mary's mantle brings us to the centrality of the *Theotokos* in Byzantine warfare and imperial politics. The relic gained great status as the city palladium (an object on which a city's safety depended) thanks to stories about it being paraded around the city walls to thwart the Avar siege in 626 and in subsequent times of danger, notably marauding Russians in 860. An early hymn claimed the city of Constantinople

> guards the precious garment of the *Theotokos*,
>
> By which [the city] is protected all the more…
>
> You have turned away my enemies and the pursuers have fled.

The mantle not only offered an impenetrable defence against enemies, but also guaranteed military victory, thus ensuring its imperial patronage. A royal palace was built near the Blachernai church for the Emperor and his entourage to use when engaged in regular processions to honour first Mary's relic and later the church's icon of the Virgin called the *Blachernitissa*.

By the 10th century, in addition to the Blachernai's custody of the mantle, the Chalkoprateia Church near Hagia Sophia claimed Mary's milk-stained girdle. Among the claimants to the Virgin's girdle today is the Vatopedi Monastery on Mt Athos in Greece. The enduring impact of Mary's relics became apparent in 2012 when, on a tour of Russia, the Vatopedi relic 'visited' Moscow's Cathedral of Christ the Saviour. This is the seat of the Russian Orthodox Patriarch, but the church also hosts prominent political events, some of them attended by Russian President Vladimir Putin. In February of 2012 the feminist punk band Pussy Riot staged a demonstration in front of the Virgin's girdle. They were immediately arrested, but, as intended, their demonstration went viral on social media. The women were protesting state censorship and the Russian Church's ties to the government, which the group accused of corruption and homophobia. The deliberately outrageous lyrics of their protest song denounced Russia's Church and government for defiling the ancient relationship between Marian relics, the Church, and state power: 'Patriarch Gundyaev believes in Putin | Bitch, better believe in God instead | The belt of the Virgin can't replace mass-meetings.' Yet their cry, 'Mary, Mother of God, is with us in protest! | Virgin Mary, Mother of God, put Putin away!' invoked the power of Mary's relics to effect miracles and restore justice, demonstrating Mary's paradoxical position at the intersection of popular veneration and official power.

Byzantine tales of Mary's mantle and other miracles spread west. At the other end of the Mediterranean, about a century after Mary's mantle arrived in Constantinople, Gregory of Tours preached in France about miracles performed by Mary's 'veil' in Constantinople. Gregory then boasted that the kingdom of the Franks could claim valuable Marian relics of its own. Medieval France's most highly prized relic was believed to be a piece of the Virgin's mantle, donated by Charles the Bald to Chartres Cathedral in 876. An image of Chartres's famous relic, identified as the tunic Mary wore in childbirth, was emblazoned on souvenir badges carried home from Chartres by medieval pilgrims.

Gregory of Tours was also the first western writer to translate Byzantine miracle tales into Latin, launching one of the most widely produced literary genres of western Christendom. Rendered into vernacular languages they became medieval best-sellers, inspiring plays, music, and the visual arts. The collections always included stories of the Virgin as intercessor, invincible defender of kings, and avenger of evil. In a popular 13th-century French collection of Mary miracle tales by Gautier de Coincy, Mary defends Constantinople by catching the attacking Muslims' catapult stones in her mantle and hurling them right back.

Icons

In the 8th and 9th centuries, as Islam consolidated its conquests, the Byzantine empire turned in on itself, expending its energies in the Iconoclast Controversy, a bitter struggle over whether religious images were permissible. Ultimately, the image advocates prevailed, arguing that because the divine had entered into the material world through the incarnation of Christ the divine must be accessible to human senses like sight and touch. Since relics provided patently material bridges between earth and heaven, they were easily accommodated within this doctrinal framework. However, the power of relics was equalled and ultimately eclipsed by painted icons. Orthodox Christians stress that because icons allow faithful viewers to encounter the divine Word, they are not painted but 'written'. By the 13th century, Byzantine icons had also inspired artists in the west to produce small-scale portable altarpieces and panels for private devotion.

In the late 10th century, icons of the Virgin took over the functions formerly played by relics: accompanying the Emperor to war, defending cities, and dominating Byzantine liturgy and processions. Also, like relics, by the 11th and 12th centuries icons were credited with all manner of wonders, from healings to public miracles. The Virgin's mantle in the Blachernai church still attracted pilgrims, but the venerable relic came to be overshadowed by an icon, the church's storied miracle-working icon of the Virgin, called *Blachernitissa* ('She of the Blachernai church') after the church to which it belonged.

The *Blachernitissa* depicted Mary with her mantle draped over her shoulders as on Kyiv's St Sofia mosaic (see Figure 5, Chapter 3), but the icon also included an image of Jesus in a medallion superimposed on Mary's chest, along the lines of the Annunciation icon from Sinai (Figure 10b). Orthodox Christians call this composition the 'Mother of God of the Sign'. By the 11th century, this icon worked a miracle every Friday, witnessed by crowds of the faithful. The Byzantine historian Michael Psellos reported that the curtain covering the icon of the Virgin 'mysteriously lifts itself up so that she would embrace inside her the entering crowd as if in a new sanctuary and inviolate refuge'. As Mary's outstretched arms enfolded the crowd, Christ's hovering presence over her womb re-enacted the incarnation before their eyes. Watching as the icon came into view, Psellos rejoiced that 'the walls separating us from the intimacy with our God' were destroyed, succinctly expressing the Orthodox belief that through icons humans experience a visible manifestation of invisible divinity.

Eventually, the most beloved of all the miracle-working icons of the Virgin was the *Hodegetria*, named for its monastery home in Constantinople. By the 12th century the *Hodegetria* had supplanted the Blachernai's mantle as the city's palladium. *Hodegetria* means 'She Who Shows the Way', and the icon depicts Mary holding Jesus on her left arm and, in an intercessory gesture, pointing toward him with her right. Jesus responds to his mother's entreaty by raising his right hand in blessing. Like the *Blachernitissa*, the *Hodegetria*'s fame was enhanced by its association with a miraculous healing Spring of the Virgin and, like the *Blachernitissa*, it offered a weekly miracle; onlookers witnessed the icon drag its bearer in circles around the monastery courtyard as if it were trying to fly through the air. The spectacle afforded miraculous healings and special blessings as the icon travelled through the city in a grand liturgical procession.

One other factor explains the *Hodegetria*'s appeal: its claim to be painted from life by St Luke. A 9th-century patriarch certified that when Mary inspected Luke's painting, she had personally endorsed it, saying, 'The grace of the one whom I bore be with it.' This legend became influential in the iconoclastic period when the *Hodegetria*'s apostolic origin and Mary's own authorization neutralized iconoclastic objections to images. Thanks to its claim to be an authentic representation of the Virgin, the *Hodegetria* became the most reproduced icon of all. Eventually hundreds of icons and some medieval statues were attributed to St Luke. Not one miracle-working icon survived Constantinople's fall in 1453, but we know what the *Hodegetria* looked like from descriptions and countless surviving copies. Orthodox Christians believe copies are as authentic as the original because icon painters are expected to use a true icon as a model with no flights of creative fancy. Thus, even a newly painted icon could claim to be a portrait by St Luke, fully imbued with divine presence.

The final icon we will consider is the *Vladimirskaya* or 'Virgin of Vladimir' (Figure 11), a type of *Hodegetria*. Currently located in Moscow's Church of St Nicholas in Tolmachi it is esteemed above all other icons in Orthodox Russia. The *Vladimirskaya* has an attribution to St Luke, too, and arrived in Kyiv, Ukraine, in 1131 as a gift from the Patriarch of Constantinople. It quickly became known as a miracle-working icon and Russians consider it their national palladium, believing that the *Vladimirskaya* has protected the motherland three times from invasion, most recently by the Nazis.

The *Vladimirskaya* is an *Eleousa* (Greek, 'tenderness') icon. The obvious affection in the tender cheek-to-cheek embrace of mother

11. Icon: *Vladimirskaya* (Virgin of Vladimir), created *c.*1130, Constantinople; sent as a gift to Russia. Church of St Nicholas in Tolmachi, Moscow.

and child illustrates a new trend toward visible emotion after Iconoclasm. Before the 10th century, Mary was usually a dignified queen seated on a jewelled throne presenting her son to the world. As in Proclus' homily, Mary's motherhood had been primarily a theological concept. Mother and Child icons had made incarnational theology visible, demonstrating that Jesus's humanity came from his mother while Mary herself remained aloof rather than exhibiting emotions in the manner of a real-life mother (see Figure 7, Chapter 3).

This new emotional turn is credited to iconophile (Greek, 'image-loving') theology: icons should present the incarnation of Christ in terms of real human emotion. It is reflected in a new title, *Meter Theou* (Greek, 'Mother of God'), that appears on the *Vladimirskaya* and other icons after Iconoclasm. By showing the love Mary feels for her child in conjunction with her foreknowledge of the Crucifixion, evident in her sombre gaze, icons expressed more fully the implications of God's incarnation as a human being. Byzantine validation of a more affective piety and its manifestation in art made a profound impression on the west, where the humanistic ethos would characterize the art, philosophy, and theology of the Renaissance.

The golden stars on the *Vladimirskaya*'s veil and shoulder are another Byzantine motif adopted in the west. They symbolize Mary's threefold virginity before, during, and after the birth of Jesus, though often, as here, the figure of Jesus overlaps one star (for all three stars, see Figure 5, Chapter 3). On the *Vladimirskaya*, however, neither the stars nor the sumptuous garments date to the 12th century. Only the faces and hands of an icon are believed capable of receiving the divine imprint and cannot be retouched; Mary's right hand has been worn down by centuries of devotion, for just as icons affirm God's love made accessible to the human world, humans may communicate their love to God not just by speech in prayer and by sight in devout contemplation but also by touching and kissing the Holy Icon. This is the paradox of icons in Orthodox practice, that they are material, sensual things that give access to the divine.

Islam

In April of 1968 the Virgin Mary appeared to a large crowd in Zeitoun, a poor neighbourhood in Cairo, Egypt. While most witnesses were Coptic Christians, many were Muslim. Between 1968 and 1971 as the apparitions continued, members of both faiths gathered for shared vigils in the courtyard of Zeitoun's Coptic Church of Mary. When they saw Mary in a light over one of the church's domes, viewers raised their hands for her intercession. Regardless of religion, most had come to ask the

Virgin for healing. Muslim witnesses to *Sitt* ('Lady') Maryam recited verses from the Qur'an as their way of asking for intercession, or even joined along with her in reciting Qur'an verses. Surveys later determined that many Muslims claimed to be recipients of Mary's miracles.

Since 2003 sectarian violence has curtailed this kind of cross-religious spirituality in much of the Middle East, but Muslim and Christian women through the centuries have rubbed shoulders at Mary's shrines and festivals all over the world. The German pilgrim Wilbrand of Oldenburg described his visit in 1212 to an image of the Virgin in Paul's hometown of Tarsus (south-western Turkey). Here, a miraculous weeping icon, 'painted by the hands of angels', was venerated by the town's mixed population of Muslims, Christians, and Jews. Historically, this has been a global phenomenon beyond the Middle East, extending into Europe, Africa, and Asia. In a recent development, immigrant Muslim women have made pilgrimages to Marian sites in Germany and Portugal in search of the same things as their Christian sisters: healing, fertility, wise counsel, and support in the face of domestic violence.

Muslims revere *Al-'Adhra'* ('the Virgin') as a model of piety, following the lead of the Prophet Muhammad who stated that Maryam was one of the four spiritually perfect women in Paradise, along with his first wife, Khadija, his daughter, Fatima, and Moses' foster mother, the Pharaoh's daughter Asiya. In the Qur'an the only Sura (chapter) named for a woman is Sura 19, 'Maryam', and she is the only woman identified by name in the Qur'an; so often, in fact, that only Moses, Abraham, and Noah outnumber her. When Muhammad cleansed the *Ka'ba* at Mecca of its reputed 360 idols, he is said to have wrapped his arms around a column decorated with a painting of Maryam and Issa (Jesus) to prevent his companions from erasing it. A minority of Muslim theologians have argued that Maryam was a prophet. *Shi'a* Muslims rank Maryam particularly highly, pairing her with Fatima as mothers of martyrs. (In 2000, the (*Shi'a*) Islamic Republic of Iran produced a

popular film, *Saint Mary*, based on the Qur'an, which may be
viewed on YouTube.)

Qur'an citations antedating any complete text of the Qur'an
appear in inscriptions dated 691–2 in Jerusalem's Dome of the
Rock. These are lines from the Qur'an that define Muslim beliefs
about Issa and Maryam and were aimed in part at the majority
Christian population of Jerusalem:

> Peace be on [Issa] the day he was born, and the day he dies, and the
> day he shall be raised alive! Such was Issa, son of Maryam, [this is]
> a statement of the truth concerning which they doubt. It does not
> befit God that He should take unto Himself a son…
>
> The Messiah, Issa son of Maryam, was only a Messenger of God,
> and His Word which He conveyed unto Maryam, and a spirit from
> Him. So, believe in God and His messengers, and say not 'Three'.

In these lines, Islam's regard for Mary and Jesus is evident, as are
beliefs shared with Christians. Issa is 'God's servant', 'Messenger'
(a title shared with Muhammad), and 'Messiah'. He rose from the dead.
Maryam is the mother of Issa who conceived God's 'Word'. Where
Muslims part company with Christians is in rejecting the Christian
doctrine of the Trinity, which Muslims consider polytheistic, as
well as the Christian belief that God could father a son.

The Qur'an's stories about Maryam and the birth of Issa in Suras 3
and 19 lie at the heart of Muslim reverence for Maryam. They share
narrative elements with a number of Christian sources—Syriac
hymns, the *Protevangelium*, and the apocryphal *Gospel of
Pseudo-Matthew*—while maintaining Islam's strict monotheism.
In Sura 3 Maryam's mother, called simply the 'wife of Imran',
dedicates her unborn child to God's service. Muslims understand
the name Maryam as meaning 'pious' or 'devoted servant of God'.
As in the *Protevangelium*, Maryam grows up in the Jerusalem
Temple where God supplies her with food from heaven.

Zakariya (Zachariah), Mary's priestly guardian in the Temple, is the father of the 'Prophet' John the Baptist whose birth is described, after which Sura 3 resumes Maryam's story. While she is in the Temple, angels come to tell her, 'God has...purified you, and chosen you.' Mary's exceptional purity was explained in a well-known hadith (an authoritative account of Muhammad's words and deeds) reported by al-Tabari, 'Not a descendant of Adam is born but he is touched by Satan...except Mary and her son.' Qur'an commentators on Maryam's purity concluded that she was preserved from all taint of imperfection including all disobedience and wrong acts, as well as, according to some interpreters, the impurity caused by menstruation. Later the angels reappear, announcing, 'Allah gives you the glad tidings of a Word from Him, his name will be the Messiah Issa.' When Maryam objects, 'O my Lord! How shall I have a son when no man has touched me?' the angels echo Gabriel's answer in Luke: 'When [Allah] has decreed something, He says to it only: "Be!" and it is.' No husband is ever mentioned in the Qur'an, but Islamic commentators explained that God chose Yusuf (Joseph) the carpenter.

The stories in Sura 19, 'Maryam', overlap slightly with Sura 3, beginning with the birth of John the Baptist followed by the Annunciation and Nativity. This Sura finds Maryam all alone when God sends his spirit, who 'appeared before her in the form of a man in all respects'. Muslims identify him as Jibril (Gabriel). Informed of the 'gift of a righteous son', Maryam asks the inevitable question: 'How can I have a son, when no man has touched me, nor am I unchaste?' Such a thing is easy for God, explains the spirit, 'So, she conceived him.' No less than Christians, Muslims wondered how Mary became pregnant. Sura 66 provides a partial answer, based on the messenger's identity as a 'spirit'. Maryam 'guarded her womb, and so We breathed into her of Our Spirit...' Commentators disagreed about the path the spirit took to Mary's womb, explaining variously that Jibril blew into the neck, sleeve, or hem of her garment or else into her mouth.

A 16th-century Persian miniature by Sadiqi Beg, head of the royal library at the Safavid Persian court, illustrates Sura 19's account of Jesus's Nativity (Figure 12). Manuscript illustration was a highly regarded artistic genre, patronized by Muslim rulers and elites from the Middle East to India between the 11th and 20th centuries. In this painting, the barren landscape reflects Sura 19's description of the 'far place' to which a pregnant Maryam withdrew, a different setting from the Christian stable or cave with Joseph in attendance. Labour pains then 'drove her to the trunk of a date-palm'. In response to Maryam's cry of distress a stream of water bubbles up, visible in the miniature in front of Maryam. A further miracle is illustrated by two bunches of dates that stand out against the golden background: a voice 'from below her', probably the newborn baby Issa, tells Maryam to 'shake the trunk

12. *Birth of Jesus in the Desert*, Sadiqi Beg, 16th century. Persian miniature depicting Jesus's nativity according to Qur'an Sura 19. Bibliothèque nationale, Paris.

of the date-palm towards you, it will let fall fresh ripe-dates upon you'. The Arabic word for 'trunk' connotes something lifeless and dry, but the tree springs to abundant life. A similar story of the infant Jesus commanding a palm tree to refresh his languishing mother appears in the *Pseudo-Gospel of Matthew*.

On the miniature, the golden flames surrounding the heads of Maryam and Issa are the Islamic equivalent of the Christian halo, while their pose and clothing resemble Christian images of the Madonna and Child. Maryam wears a headcloth, long veil, and a blue cloak (mantle) over a red dress. The golden background, too, is familiar from Byzantine icons. As for the menacing figure lurking behind the rock, he is most likely Satan, illustrating Muhammad's assertion that Satan could not touch Mary and Jesus.

As Sura 19 continues, Maryam must keep a vow of silence, a distinct problem when she arrives home with a newborn. The townsfolk accuse her of immorality, and in her defence Maryam can only point to her child. This episode has affinities with a 5th-century Syriac Christian dialogue hymn in which Mary worries, 'There will be a great commotion concerning me; … I shall be accounted an adulteress, and if my Son does not look after me, I shall be torn to pieces.' The infant Issa does indeed 'look after' his mother. When Maryam's neighbours scoff, 'How can we talk to one who is a child in the cradle?' the newborn Issa speaks out in his mother's defence, then announces, 'I am a slave of Allah, He has given me the Scripture and made me a Prophet.'

As early as the 10th century, Muslim pilgrims to the *Haram al-Sharif* (Arabic, 'Noble Sanctuary', Jerusalem's Temple Mount) prayed in the Mosque of Mary located in the underground hall known to Crusaders as the Stables of Solomon. Pilgrims were shown the cradle from which Jesus spoke. Muslim pilgrims also visited the Church of the Nativity in Bethlehem to pray at the place Issa was born. A 13th-century treaty between the Egyptian

Sultan and the Holy Roman Emperor ensured that Muslims would 'have free access to the cathedral at Bethlehem'. In Lebanon today, Christians and Muslims enjoy the seasonal tradition of outdoor Nativity scenes even in the centre of majority Muslim Beirut.

For conservative Muslims, Maryam conforms to patriarchal gender norms as a submissive, veiled, devout mother. Yet the Muslim women who travel to Christian Mary shrines often do so in quiet defiance of Muslim authorities—all men—who prohibit the veneration of saints. They go because they believe *Sitt* Maryam hears and helps.

Chapter 6
Empress of heaven and hell: Mary in the Middle Ages and Renaissance

Notre-Dame de Paris. Notre-Dame de Chartres. Notre-Dame de Senlis. As the names of these and other Gothic cathedrals suggest—*Notre Dame* is French for 'Our Lady'—whether as a Mediatrix, Queen, Mother of Sorrows, Mother of Mercy, or simply Mother, the Virgin Mary came into her own in the 11th and 12th centuries, Europe's High Middle Ages. Between 1150 and 1250, over 80 cathedrals and 500 churches were erected in honour of the Virgin Mary and by the 15th century most churches could claim a miracle-working image of Mary. In 1904, overwhelmed by his encounter with the Virgin in Gothic churches, Boston historian Henry Adams famously wrote, 'Symbol or energy, the Virgin had acted as the greatest force the western world ever felt, and had drawn man's activities to herself more strongly than any other power, natural or supernatural, had ever done.' The same Marian energy carried over into the Renaissance (roughly 1300–1550) when Jesus's humanity, secured by Mary's motherhood, became the touchstone for the humanist temper of the age.

Even before 1054, when a disagreement about the Trinity split Christianity into Orthodox and Catholic, the west had been following its own path. Nowhere is this clearer than with regard to the Byzantine iconoclastic era when in the west the Carolingian Church under Charlemagne and his dynasty (750–887) continued to create religious images. After Iconoclasm, the west continued to follow Byzantine trends, especially Byzantine artists' depiction of human emotion, but western independence is apparent in Romanesque art and architecture and, above all, in sculpture. Sculptures of the Virgin and Child became widespread in Europe in the 12th century, beginning with the seated Romanesque Throne of Wisdom figures discussed earlier.

Carolingian scholars translated Greek works into Latin, including what would become the most famous medieval Marian legend (discussed below). Charlemagne modelled his own Palatine Chapel directly on the 6th-century Byzantine church of San Vitale in Ravenna and dedicated both it and his realm's most important church, Aix-la-Chapelle, to the Virgin. Important Latin hymns to the Virgin date to this period, among them *Salve Regina* ('Hail, O Queen') and the Advent antiphon, *Alma Redemptoris Mater* ('Loving Mother of the Redeemer'), although the earliest and most popular hymn was the 10th-century *Ave Maris Stella*, 'Hail Star of the Sea'. These are Latin songs, but many of Mary's titles—including Star of the Sea—as well as songs beginning with a salutation to Mary (such as *Salve!* and *Ave!*) ultimately derive from the Byzantine *Akathistos* hymn.

A variety of factors contributed to the explosion of Marian devotion in medieval and Renaissance spirituality. Medieval Christians tended to see Christ as sternly judgemental and Mary as merciful. Entering cathedral doorways, worshippers often encountered stern images of Christ enthroned in majesty or in judgement. Mary, on the other hand, represented infinite mercy. Closer to eye level on cathedral entryways, sculptures of the Virgin show her gazing or smiling sweetly at her infant son, reminding the faithful of her maternal influence with Jesus, assuring them of her effective intercession. A text attributed to the scholastic theologian Bonaventure explained that 'The blessed Virgin chose the best part, because she was made Queen of Mercy, while her Son remained King of Justice; and mercy is better than justice.'

For Bonaventure, salvation depended on Mary's intercession: 'No one enters heaven except through her... hence the Lord never receives anyone without her mediation.'

Mary's intercession with Christ acquired new urgency with a change in expectations about the soul's fate after death. Prior to the 12th century, the dominant belief was that souls would be resurrected and judged at the end of time. Now, Christians in the west had come to believe that souls were judged right after death. Martyrs went straight to heaven, but everyone else had to spend time in Purgatory to 'purge' their remaining sins. Only after all sins were burned away, as fire purifies metal, could the soul enter heaven. One's time in Purgatory could be reduced by Masses and by the prayers of the living that could earn indulgences (Church-approved reductions of time in Purgatory). Prayers to the Virgin Mary, the greatest intercessor, were an important feature of this balance sheet of sin and salvation.

Monastic reforms in the 11th and 12th centuries raised the education level of monks and nuns and encouraged a practice of meditation and prayer that brought Mary more affectively and effectively into their devotions. Daily prayers were shaped by the *Little Office of the Virgin*, the core text of late medieval Books of Hours. Even illiterate Christians could recite portions of the *Little Office* by heart, especially the leading medieval prayer, the *Ave Maria*: 'Hail, Mary, full of grace, the Lord is with thee. Blessed art thou amongst women and blessed is the fruit of thy womb.'

The 13th century also saw the remarkable success of the Franciscans and Dominicans, preaching orders ministering to the physical and spiritual needs of lay Christians, particularly the poor and lowborn. Franciscans encouraged devotions in front of images and expressed a special, sometimes quite extravagant love of the Virgin. One of the most popular Franciscan preachers, Bernardino of Siena, expressed his opinion that 'the Blessed Virgin was able to do more for God than God could do for himself'. And it was

St Francis who is credited with inventing the Christmas crèche to remind Christians of Christ's poverty and humility. Reportedly, worshippers knelt by a hay-lined manger alongside the ox and ass. Franciscan and Dominican piety is also reflected in the 'Madonna of Humility', a type of Virgin that appeared in 14th-century painting. Possibly influenced by Islamic art, this less regal Mary sits on the ground rather than a throne. She may have angelic attendants, but in some cases, she is emphatically down-to-earth, sitting in a field or garden. In the Reformation this more modest vision of Mary was championed by Martin Luther.

St Francis shared his profound conviction of God's love by example and in everyday language. The influential 12th-century Cistercian preacher and scholar Bernard of Clairvaux drew on his rich knowledge of scripture to teach, like St Francis, that faith should be immediate and personal and that Christians had no greater mediator than the Virgin Mary. Bernard's writings on Mary earned him the nickname, 'Troubadour of Mary'. His celebrated Advent homily 'In Praise of the Virgin Mary' echoed the lyrics of *Ave Maris Stella*:

> . . . do not turn your eyes away from this shining star, unless you want to be overwhelmed by the hurricane. If temptation storms, or you fall upon the rocks of tribulation, look to the star: Call upon Mary!

Fulbert of Chartres, preaching in physical proximity to France's principal miracle-working Marian relic, the 'chemise' of the Virgin, echoed the common 11th-century conviction that 'Jesus accorded his mother more honour than any other saint and owed her his obedience.' Medieval story collections called legendaries— collections of saints' lives—popularized Marian tales from the *Protevangelium* and other apocryphal texts. Celebrating the relatively new (and non-biblical) feast of the Virgin's Nativity, Fulbert endorsed the Church's greater openness to apocryphal accounts of Mary's life, arguing that 'particularly on this day it seemed that the book that was found written concerning [Mary's] origin and life ought to be read in church, even though the [Church] Fathers did not decide to include it'. 'Mary's faithful children' demanded it, he insisted.

Latin versions of apocryphal stories gained credibility by attribution to ancient authors. The *Gospel of Pseudo-Matthew* claimed Matthew as its author. The Dormition account in the *Transitus of Pseudo-Melito* was associated with Augustine. Arguably the most influential legendary was the *Golden Legend*, a genuine medieval best-seller compiled around 1260 by the Dominican Jacob of Voragine. The *Golden Legend*'s compendious selection of saints' lives inspired countless medieval and Renaissance artworks. Prelates and religious orders, wealthy merchants and nobles freely commissioned altarpieces and private devotional works based on episodes from the apocrypha.

The most popular Mary miracle story was the 'Legend of Theophilus' which appears in countless sermons and Books of Hours and became the basis for the Faust legend. It contains the earliest Latin reference to Mary as 'Mediatrix' between God and humanity and demonstrated that Mary's authority extended not just up to heaven but also down to Hell. In the story, Theophilus is a disgruntled 6th-century Byzantine cleric who, on the advice of a 'Jewish lawyer', sells his soul to the Devil and signs the contract with his blood. When a panic-stricken Theophilus repents, Mary sternly scolds him, but then reveals she has convinced God to pardon him. Unfortunately, Theophilus tells Mary, he still needs to get his blood-inscribed document back from the Devil. Three days later Theophilus has his contract back. Mary had travelled to hell and wrested the document out of Satan's hands.

Episodes from the Theophilus legend were pictured in manuscripts, stained-glass windows, and in a rare sculpted version preserved on the north transept doorway at Notre-Dame in Paris where Mary brandishes a sword over a cowering Devil.

Mary's persona in the Theophilus story is typical of her miracle stories. She is a fearless guardian of her devotees and an implacable punisher of her foes. Her power over the Devil also explains one of her more surprising medieval titles, Empresse of Helle.

In the 14th century, new types of devotion spread across Europe aimed at individual cultivation of piety by ordinary people. One technique involved meditative visualization in which a devotee sought to experience what we might today call virtual reality, becoming present at biblical events like the Nativity or the Passion of Christ. Empathetic identification with Jesus and Mary deepened one's love of God, refined the soul, and brought salvation closer; ideally, it inspired a more sanctified life in this world. The hugely popular spiritual biography, *Meditations on the Life of Christ*, was written to guide a Franciscan nun through this type of meditation, encouraging imaginative licence within the bounds of orthodoxy. While narrating the life of Christ, the author takes on the role of a meditation coach. For example, the Annunciation story begins, 'Here, too, watch closely, as if you were actually present...O what a little house...' At the Nativity, the reader is encouraged to kiss the Baby Jesus's 'little feet'. One late medieval meditative practice encouraged systematic meditation on the body parts of Christ and Mary with particular attention to the Virgin's beauty: 'O sweet Mary, your cheeks were of the best complexion, white and red. God was very pleased with your beauty and never turned his eyes from you.'

Works of art enriched this devotional trend. Just as contemplating images of the Nativity could evoke joy and wonder, being fully present at the Passion meant sharing Mary's heartbreak and Jesus's agony. For private devotion, half-length portraits of the suffering Virgin or *Mater Dolorosa* (Latin, 'Sorrowful Mother') were paired with Jesus as the 'Man of Sorrows' displaying his wounds. Contrasting with Mary's youthful beauty, the *Mater Dolorosa* appeared aged, with ravaged features bearing stark testimony to the trauma of watching her son die on the cross. The sorrowful Mary also appeared in the *Pietà*, a sculptural image that originated in Germany around 1300 and spread all over Europe. Conventionally, a *Pietà* consists of the dead Christ draped over Mary's lap, a tragic inversion of the Madonna cradling her infant son.

By the 12th century, western artists inspired by Byzantine images of Mary swooning at the Crucifixion were creating their own variation in which Mary collapses in the arms of her companions. Initially, church officials objected to this emotional display as unworthy of Mary; they maintained that the Virgin displayed steadfast faith at the Crucifixion, standing resolutely, sorrowful but dry-eyed. Nevertheless, Mary's swoon figured prominently in devotional texts and countless Crucifixion scenes. Many devotees in the later Middle Ages and Renaissance would have experienced these Crucifixion scenes through the affective lens of the *Stabat Mater*, the familiar medieval Latin hymn which began, 'The sorrowful mother stood weeping beside the cross while her son was hanging', and included the plea, 'Yea Mother, fountain of love, make me feel the power of sorrow that I may grieve with you.'

Mary's anguish at the cross also came to be viewed as the fulfilment of Simeon's enigmatic prophecy in Luke 2:35 that 'a sword will pierce your own soul too'. Her distress was also linked to the notion that Mary, the new Eve, had been exempt from Eve's punishment of pain in childbirth. Instead, according to the 12th-century theologian Rupert of Deutz, it was beside the cross that Mary was 'truly a mother and at this hour, she truly suffers the pains of childbirth. When [Jesus] was born, she did not suffer like other mothers: now, however, she suffers, she is tormented and full of sorrow, because her hour has come.' Rupert shared with many medieval Christians the belief that human salvation was achieved thanks to the suffering of both Jesus and Mary. His *Commentary on the Gospel of John* explains, 'in the Passion of her only Son, the Blessed Virgin gave birth to the salvation of all mankind: in effect, she is the mother of all mankind'.

Mary's book

Byzantine Annunciation icons showed Mary spinning the veil of the Temple, a scene from the *Protevangelium* which enjoyed scriptural status in the Orthodox east (see Figure 10a, Chapter 5). By the 12th century in the west, the Annunciate Mary was not shown spinning but alone in her room with a book. On one level, Mary's book was a reminder of the familiar incarnational theme of Mary conceiving Jesus as the Word of God. Yet this version of the Annunciation had no scriptural or artistic precedent. In part, Mary's reading reflects contemporary reality. Female literacy increased through the Middle Ages, first in cloisters, which multiplied tenfold, and then among lay women. It is not a coincidence that this is the period when images of St Anne teaching the Virgin Mary to read made their appearance. Women owned and read Books of Hours, prayer books, saints' lives like the *Golden Legend*, and spiritual guides like the *Meditations*. Medieval women, like the intended reader of the *Meditations*, would see themselves mirrored in Mary, the model Christian female reader.

Nevertheless, the image of a solitary Mary reading in an enclosed room appears to have originated in the male monastic world before it appeared in painting and the stained-glass windows of cathedrals (some of the earliest at Chartres in 1145). Carolingian religious reforms had demanded male clerical literacy for the Divine Office and for contemplation of the scriptures. Among monastics, Mary was accorded all the virtues of a model monk. Not only had she made a vow of virginity (a notion that dated back to the Church Fathers), but she also dedicated her solitary hours to prayerful study of scripture. Thus the *Meditations* suggest that when Gabriel appears for the Annunciation, he finds Mary 'shut up in her private room praying or in her meditations or perhaps reading the prophecy of Isaiah about the Incarnation'. She was a scholar, ultimately crowned by the medieval Scholastics as the queen of the Trivium, the three primary disciplines of grammar, logic, and rhetoric.

According to Athanasius' 4th-century *First Letter to Virgins*, Mary had studied the scriptures. Now, in the *Gospel of Pseudo-Matthew*, medieval readers learnt of Mary that 'there was no one more learned in the wisdom of the law of God [i.e. the Bible], more humble in humility, more elegant in the songs of David [i.e. Psalms]'. When you encounter a Renaissance painting of the Annunciation, look for Mary's book. You may be able to decipher the text she is reading, and chances are good you will see the Latin word *Ecce* ('Behold') the first word of Isaiah 7:14: *'Ecce virgo concipiet'* ('Behold, a virgin will conceive').

Mary's body

The Church Fathers struggled to imagine the physical process involved in Christ's conception. Because Mary's breast milk held such theological significance, it was probably inevitable that theologians found themselves considering Mary's body according to the gynaecology of their time. Aristotelian science taught that during pregnancy menstrual blood was retained to feed the foetus and then, in the agitation of childbirth, the blood churned into white foam to become breast milk. Thomas Aquinas pronounced that because Mary had nursed Jesus and was human herself, she must have menstruated, but with the qualification that her uniquely pure menstrual blood never needed to be shed in a period. Menstruation had been associated with the curse of Eve since Patristic times, and the nature of Mary's bodily purity would become particularly fraught in debates over her Immaculate Conception.

Like Ephraim of Syria, who had called the Eucharist 'grape from Mary' in his *Hymns for the Unleavened Bread*, medieval theologians found meaningful parallels between the blood of Mary and that of her son. They taught that Jesus's eucharistic blood was doubly derived from Mary: first from her womb and then from her breasts. Renaissance artists illustrated this eucharistic equivalency in the 'Double Intercession', a variant of the 'Madonna of Mercy' in which Mary shields sinners beneath her famous mantle. The 'Double Intercession' depicted Jesus and Mary before a stern God the Father (sometimes armed with bristling arrows) while Mary bares her breast and Jesus points to the bleeding wound in his chest. Together they intercede for the supplicants kneeling under and around Mary's cloak.

Medieval gynaecology also taught that to conceive a child, the woman must experience orgasm. While Aquinas stressed that Mary's menstrual blood was unsullied by any of the sin-laden lust that normally fuelled orgasmic conception, medieval authors of Marian texts did not shy away from imagining Mary's ecstasy at the Annunciation. In language that would characterize later Catholic mystics' beatific encounter with the divine, Rupert of Deutz described Mary's conception of Jesus in terms of the lover's rapturous kiss in the Song of Songs 1:1,

> O blessed Mary, the inundation of joy, the force of love, the torrent
> of delight, covered you entirely, possessed you totally, intoxicated
> you inwardly, and you sensed what eye has not seen and ear has not
> heard and what has not entered into the heart of man, and you said,
> 'Let him kiss me with the kiss of his mouth.'

Popular affection for Mary is apparent in the ribald situations and language of medieval mystery plays which often treat Mary as if she were a beloved sister ripe for teasing. In the topsy-turvy of a carnival setting, medieval re-enactments of scenes from the life of Mary and Jesus could include transgressive episodes with Mary accused of licentiousness, publicly tested for her virginity, and even seducing God. One English mystery play, *Joseph's Doubt*, has a highly suspicious Joseph accuse his wife's handmaiden-chaperones of either covering up for their pregnant mistress or falling down on the job. Joseph scoffs at the maidens' lame claim that an angel had visited their mistress when *he* knows that 'some man in an angel's likeness' sneaked into his wife's bedroom. The joke, however, is ultimately on the Devil, since the audience is never in doubt about Mary's innocence, while the Devil is tricked into thinking Mary and her child Jesus are already sinners and are not worth his attention.

Joseph was also a favourite target of bawdy jokes which invariably cast him as an elderly cuckold, the husband of an unfaithful wife. Yet, as God's cuckold, Joseph has his own part to play in God's plan of salvation, as unique in its way as the virginal conception. Through laughter and tears an unschooled audience absorbed doctrinal principles: God's plan of salvation, Mary's role as the New Eve and human mother of Jesus, and the physical reality of Jesus's suffering.

Mary and anti-Judaism

From today's perspective, the truly 'dark side' of medieval Marian miracle stories and rowdy mystery plays is not the irreverence, nor the cheerful amorality that assured all sinners—from errant nuns to rank evildoers—that an appeal to Mary would bring reprieve from otherwise inevitable punishment. The dark side is anti-Judaism, the routine association of Jews with the Devil as exemplified in the Theophilus legend. So familiar were Marian miracle stories like that of Theophilus that prayer books and Books of Hours could dispense with text and simply include illustrations full of inflammatory but instantly recognizable anti-Jewish scenes of Jewish ritual murder, cannibalism, and host desecration.

Christian anti-Judaism was already a factor in the Gospels even though the Jewishness of Jesus, all the apostles, and the Virgin Mary was never in doubt. That Mary was Jewish was also clear in the Apocrypha, especially the *Protevangelium*. Christians were taught that Mary was descended from Abraham and David, grew up in the Jewish Temple, and helped make the Temple curtain. Luke shows Mary joining in Jewish rituals like the circumcision of her son, her post-partum purification, and the Passover. Yet in an ironic twist of fate, Mary's Jewishness provided the fulcrum for Christians to express fear and hatred of Jews. Christians believed that Jews' own scriptures promised the Messiah would be born from a virgin, so when Jews refused to acknowledge Mary's virginal conception of Jesus, Christians took what they perceived as Jewish obstinacy as a threat to Christianity itself. For Christians, Mary was a Jewish girl who became a model Christian and embodied the principle of Christian supersessionism, the belief that Christ's Crucifixion and Resurrection rendered Judaism null and void.

These two factors, Jewish disbelief and Christian supersessionism, are apparent in one of the first anti-Jewish Marian stories: the Dormition account of hostile Jews attacking Mary's dead body only to be blinded and maimed before they convert. Jewish disbelief and Christian supersessionism also underlie the deliberately anti-Jewish timing of Mary's earliest known feast day; the Jerusalem Church's 15 August commemoration of Mary's Holy Maternity coincided with *Tisha b'Av* when Jews mourned the destruction of the Temple. (Celebrating Mary's Assumption on 15 August came later.) Hesychius, a Jerusalem church elder, preached a 15 August sermon which described Mary as 'another Temple larger than heaven', implicitly dismissing the Jewish Temple as superseded. Anti-Semitic passages are common in Syriac and Byzantine writings about Mary, including miracle stories like the Theophilus legend. A favourite Byzantine miracle tale adopted in the west told of a Jew who stole an icon of Mary and hid it in a latrine. The Devil kills the Jew, whose body disappears forever, after which a Christian retrieves the icon which still smells sweeter than all the perfumes of the east.

Christian antagonism toward Jews erupted into widespread violence in the 12th and 13th centuries, just when the Cult of the Virgin came to dominate Europe. When Crusaders set out in 1090 for the Holy Land, Christians slipped all too easily into militaristic thinking, indiscriminately lumping Jews and Muslims together as enemies in a Holy War that encouraged Christians to kill the 'Infidel'. Unprecedented massacres of Jewish communities accompanied the Crusaders across Europe. Bernard of Clairvaux was in the minority in calling for peace with Jews, although his intent was that they be kept alive to be converted. The new devotional techniques and writings that encouraged Christians to contemplate Christ's Passion led Christians in their imaginations through the events of the Crucifixion in excruciating detail, usually with intensely negative portrayals of Jews. Thus, an activity meant to foster Christian compassion often generated an equal and opposite reaction of animosity against Jews, identified as the killers of Mary's beloved son, Jesus.

Jews were also scapegoats when the Black Death erupted in the 14th century, and they were not helped by the pervasive belief in Christian Europe that Jews allied with demonic powers to threaten the health and safety of Christian communities. In Marian miracle stories Jews were carnal, demonic, and associated with bodily waste, while Mary was the opposite. Christians turned to Mary to keep the Devil at bay, knowing she would not shy from the most sordid circumstances when her help was needed. As the Theophilus legend claimed, a Jew in league with the Devil might get you in trouble, but the Empresse of Helle could be counted on to beat the Devil and the Jews at their own game.

Mary's Assumption

By the 12th century the western Church was celebrating five Marian feasts, all adopted from Constantinople and Jerusalem. Two were based on the Gospel of Luke: the Annunciation (15 March) and Mary's Purification (2 February), and three were apocryphal: the Virgin's Nativity (8 September), Assumption (15 August), and Presentation in the Temple (21 November). Liturgical readings for Mary's Nativity highlighted God's plan of salvation by including Isaiah's prophecy ('a virgin shall conceive and bear a son and call his name Emmanuel') and Matthew's genealogy of Jesus. Because these were also Christmas texts, parallels were established between the births of Mary and Jesus. Corresponding with these biblical texts were legendaries that told of Mary's miraculous birth and credited her with illustrious Davidic and Levitic (priestly) ancestry.

The Feast of the Assumption commemorated the end of Mary's life and her elevation to heaven as recounted in Dormition narratives that by 1100 had appeared in sixty different versions and at least nine languages. Orthodox liturgy incorporated apocryphal Dormition texts, but this was not the case in the west, even though a version of the Dormition circulated widely in the Latin *Transitus of Pseudo-Melito*. In the 9th century the Carolingian Church baulked at memorializing the end of Mary's life, citing the lack of Marian bodily relics that guaranteed the necessary link to heaven and saintly intercession. In fact, many churchmen in the west expressed hope that Mary's body might yet be discovered. By the 12th century, popular demand and the appearance of a treatise on the Assumption attributed to Augustine (but actually a 9th-century work) brought Mary's Assumption into the festal cycle. Paris's Notre-Dame cathedral was even dedicated to the Assumption of the Virgin. How Mary's body and soul came together remained unclear, but no one doubted that Mary reigned as *Regina Caeli*, queen of heaven.

Christians attending church on a saint's day expected to hear stories about the saint. Readings for the Feast of the Assumption included passages from the Song of Songs and Revelation 12. (Confusingly, the Song of Songs has alternative titles: Canticle of Canticles and the Song of Solomon.) Originally these texts had nothing to do with the Virgin or her Assumption. The Song of

Songs is a collection of ancient Israelite love lyrics exchanged by unmarried lovers. However, taking their cue from Jewish rabbis, Christian theologians read the lyrics allegorically as declarations of love between God and the Church or between God and the individual Christian soul. By the 12th century a complex process of interpretative evolution influenced by Pseudo-Melito's Dormition narrative turned the Song of Songs into a dialogue between Jesus and Mary, beginning at her deathbed and ending in heaven, where the Bridegroom Jesus welcomes his Bride Mary. While Mary prepares for death, Christ calls to Mary, 'Now the winter has passed, the rain has gone and departed, rise, my beloved and come!' (Song 2:11). Arising from her bed, Mary exults, 'His left arm under my head, his right arm will embrace me' (Song 2:6; 8:3). The *Golden Legend*'s account of Mary's coronation quoted the Feast of the Assumption reading from Song 4:8 in which Jesus addresses Mary,

> 'Come my chosen and I shall set you upon my throne...Come from Lebanon, my spouse, come from Lebanon; thou shalt be crowned.'...And so, rejoicing, she was taken into heaven and seated on a throne of glory to the right of her son.

Above the doorways of Gothic cathedrals, the words from the Song of Songs were visualized as Mary and Jesus enthroned side by side like a Bride and Bridegroom, reassuring viewers of what they heard from preachers like Philip of Harvengt: 'Therefore the Bride is rightly called the mediatress of us all...because...asking her Spouse and commanding her Son she turns his fury into grace and his wrath into sweetest love.' Sometimes they embrace like lovers, as in the spectacular 12th-century mosaic in the Church of Santa Maria in Trastevere in Rome, and sometimes Christ (or the Trinity) crowns Mary. By the 15th century, the erotic imagery of the Song of Songs and Marian adoration had influenced imaginings of the Annunciation as well. The Franciscan preacher Bernardino of Siena spoke rapturously of Mary seducing God before she conceived Jesus:

O the unthinkable power of the Virgin Mother!...One Hebrew
woman invaded the house of the eternal King; one girl, I do not
know by what caresses, pledges or violence, seduced, deceived, and
if I may say so, wounded and enraptured the divine heart and
ensnared the Wisdom of God...

If at the Assumption Mary and her son become bride and
bridegroom as well as brother and sister, we are faced with the
troubling question of incest. Strict rules about incest in medieval
canon law banned marriage between people related by up to seven
degrees and even between unrelated children who shared the
same wet nurse. However, theologians stressed that the love of
Mary and Jesus was unique in encompassing and transcending
human love and confounding the capabilities of human language.
How better to express some measure of this love than by turning
to the Bible and the luminous language of the Song of Songs?

In contrast to Gothic Assumption images with Mary seated on a
throne, Renaissance artists showed Mary kneeling at the feet of
Jesus or the Trinity to be crowned. The relatively static heavenly
coronations of Gothic art also gave way in the Renaissance to
dramatic scenes of Mary's Assumption to heaven. These were
more dynamic vertical compositions with the Apostles attending
Mary's Dormition in the lower portion and then looking upward
at Mary floating up to heaven. This celestial Assumption imagery
was based on Revelation 12's account of 'a woman clothed with the
sun, with the moon under her feet, and on her head a crown of
twelve stars'.

Art accommodated theological doctrine and popular belief alike.
Assumption and coronation scenes demonstrate the west's
increasing independence from Orthodox Marian prototypes and
theology. For example, Orthodox art never depicts any heavenly
ascent or coronation of Mary though she may wear a crown while
holding the infant Jesus. In Byzantine Dormitions and early

western Assumption scenes, the Apostles and Jesus surround the clearly dead Mary lying on her bier and, in a surprising reversal of the traditional Madonna and Child motif, Jesus holds Mary's infant-like soul in his arms. When the Catholic Church determined that Mary had risen to heaven in both body and soul, the separate figure of Mary's tiny soul was no longer considered appropriate, and Byzantine-style Dormition deathbed scenes disappeared.

Assumption scenes now showed the startled Apostles looking up at the figure of Mary surrounded by clouds and angels, most famously in Titian's high altarpiece of 1518 in Venice's Church of the Frari. Early renditions of the Assumption often included an empty sarcophagus beneath the ascending Virgin to show that she had died then risen on the third day, leaving behind an empty tomb just like Jesus. In time, however, the sarcophagus disappeared or was only hinted at, reflecting Catholic ambivalence over whether or not Mary had actually died. For medieval Christians, however, belief in Mary's Assumption did more than provide tangible reassurance of the eventual resurrection of their own bodies and souls. Her physical proximity to God in heaven assured the faithful that Mary's pleas on their behalf would be heard.

One popular tradition reflected in Italian paintings of the Assumption illustrates the origin of one of Italy's greatest relics, the *Sacra Cintola* (Italian, 'sacred belt'). Mary's girdle or belt is still the pride of the Tuscan city of Prato. (Prato's belt rivals other claimants including the Orthodox Vatopedi belt relic discussed earlier.) In these paintings, the Virgin, already airborne, drops her belt down to the Apostle ('Doubting') Thomas who had arrived late for the Dormition. The scene reinforced the material reality of the Assumption event and the relic. Mary's maternity is linked with the Assumption belt story in 14th-century Tuscan paintings of the *Madonna del Parto* (Figure 13), a heavily pregnant

13. *Madonna del Parto* (Pregnant Madonna), Piero della Francesca, *c.*1460, Monterchi, Italy. Fresco, commissioned for the altar of a village chapel. Flanked by angels, Mary stands inside a goat-skin tent. Mary, visibly pregnant with Jesus, 'the Word [of God] made flesh' (John 1:14), symbolizes the biblical Ark of the Covenant (Exodus 25), the box which contained the Ten Commandments (i.e. God's word). The Ark of the Covenant was similarly flanked by Cherubim and kept within the goat-skin Tabernacle (tent).

Madonna wearing the *Sacra Cintola*. Although St Margaret was the official patron of childbirth, women in labour also called on the Virgin who could, as was St Bridget's experience, ease a difficult labour. Women were encouraged to touch the *Sacra Cintola* with a girdle of their own and during childbirth to lay it across their bellies to assure a safe and easy delivery.

The Immaculate Conception

When Fulbert preached his sermon for the Nativity of the Virgin, he stressed Mary's essential role in God's plan of salvation by citing Old Testament prophetic texts that Christians associated with Mary, such as Isaiah 7's 'a virgin shall conceive' and Isaiah 11, which promised that a branch would sprout from the tree stump of Jesse, King David's father. Another favourite Marian text was Genesis 3:15, where God promises that Eve's offspring would strike the serpent's head. In the Hebrew text of Genesis, Eve's offspring is male, but Jerome's Latin translation uses the feminine pronoun, 'she', which was read as a 'New Eve' prophecy. In other words, Mary as Eve's offspring would defeat the Devil (the serpent) by giving birth to Jesus. This Marian interpretation of the Latin text of Genesis 3:15 explains why there is a snake—symbolizing the Devil—under Mary's feet in images of the Immaculate Conception such as the *Miraculous Medal* (see Figure 1).

Centuries of sometimes bitter debate preceded Pope Pius IX's 1854 declaration of the Immaculate Conception, that the 'Virgin Mary, in the first instance of her conception...was preserved free from all stain of original sin.' The Immaculate Conception controversy arose first in England, which had adopted the Byzantine feast of Mary's conception in the early 11th century only to see it suppressed after the Norman conquest of 1066. In protest, English theologians wrote treatises justifying the feast and articulating the unique nature of Mary's conception. Many theologians objected to the feast because honouring the conception of a saint contradicted the tradition of celebrating a saint's death date as her spiritual birthday. Both the feast and the nature of Mary's conception became a central theological issue of the late 12th and 13th centuries; the Franciscans supported it, while Dominicans and Cistercians did not.

For centuries the Church had affirmed that Mary never sinned. At issue was precisely *when* in her life she was freed from original sin.

From Ephraim of Syria in the 4th century to Anselm of Canterbury in the late 11th, many theologians believed that Mary was freed from original sin by being 'baptized' or 'sanctified' at the Annunciation. Anselm's pupil, Eadmer, however, argued that God would never have waited so long to purify the mother of Christ; God must have sanctified Mary at her conception. Sanctification in the womb was not a new idea. Christians believed John the Baptist was cleansed of original sin at the Visitation when he leapt for joy in Elizabeth's womb (Luke 1:44). Eastern Christians celebrated the birthdays of two saints, the *Theotokos* and John the Baptist, the only humans who were cleansed of sin before the birth of Christ, a gesture of divine grace that warranted their unique powers of intercession. Even today Orthodox Christians invoke 'Mary interceding together with John the Baptist', as they pray before the *Deesis* icon (Figure 14) of Christ flanked by the supplicating figures of the *Theotokos* and the 'Blessed Forerunner', John the Baptist. In the early 14th century John Duns Scotus, a Franciscan, articulated the scenario in his *Four Questions on Mary* that explained the west's view of the Immaculate Conception: Mary was conceived in the normal way, but Christ as the perfect Redeemer was capable of preserving Mary from original sin at the moment of her conception, because 'redemption that preserves from sin is more perfect than one that frees from it'.

Female visionaries played a prominent part in the dispute over the Immaculate Conception. The 14th-century Franciscan St Bridget of Sweden reported that Mary had explained that because Anna and Joachim could only be persuaded to break their mutual vow of virginity by God's command, the intercourse that conceived Mary was divinely consecrated (*Revelation* 6). But St Bridget's Dominican contemporary, St Catherine of Siena, reportedly claimed Mary had insisted she was not immaculately conceived. By the later Middle Ages the feast of the Immaculate Conception had such broad support, however, that the Franciscan Pope Sixtus IV endorsed the feast in 1476, although he was also compelled in

14. *'Deesis'* (Greek, 'prayer'). Traditional Byzantine Orthodox image of Christ in heaven flanked by the Virgin Mary and John the Baptist who raise their hands in supplication on behalf of humans.

the 1480s to insist that the Franciscans and Dominicans cease accusing each other of heresy over the issue.

Theology and popular enthusiasm for Mary's Immaculate Conception visibly coalesced in religious art. Giotto's frescos for the Franciscan Arena Chapel (1305) in Padua, Italy, are often considered the starting point of Renaissance art. Giotto included scenes from the Infancy of Mary, a new decorative series that bolstered Franciscan advocacy of Mary's Immaculate Conception; many

Franciscans condoned the popular notion (ultimately condemned by Pope Innocent XI in 1677) that Mary was miraculously conceived when Anna and Joachim kissed at the Golden Gate of Jerusalem rather than through any sexual intercourse which would have exposed her to original sin. Giotto's sympathetic portrayal of the elderly couple's mutual affection is regularly invoked to illustrate the Renaissance's new embrace of the human.

The Cistercian Bernard, and others who denied anything more miraculous about Mary's conception than her parents' advanced age, warned that suggesting Anna and Joachim's conception of Mary was a holy act would be the thin edge of the wedge, necessitating an infinite regression of miraculous conceptions without sexual intercourse. By the 13th century Bernard's prediction had come true in the form of verse tales on sacred subjects inspired by successful secular romances about heroes like King Arthur. The new 'sacred romances' were written for popular consumption, putting fantasy first and theology second, and like their secular counterparts they delighted in detailed genealogies. The French *Roman de St Fanuel* about Mary's maternal ancestors begins with an unnamed daughter of Abraham who conceived by inhaling the perfume of the Tree of Life, a seedling of which grew in Abraham's garden. Mary's grandfather, Fanuel, rubbed juice from the fruit of the same tree on his thigh inside which Anna then gestated like Dionysus in the thigh of Zeus. The *Roman*'s author insisted that the Virgin could boast a human bloodline wholly untainted by sex or sin.

The Immaculate Conception also contributed to the popularity of St Anne (Anna). In family portraits of Jesus's maternal line, called the 'Holy Kinship', the infant Jesus appeared with his grandmother Anna and his mother Mary, the fruit of Anna's womb. The Holy Kinship not only illustrated God's plan of salvation working its way through the generations, but also visualized an abstract concept like the Immaculate Conception by calling attention to divinely sanctified motherhood. Leonardo da Vinci's *Madonna and Child with St Anne* is perhaps the best-known version of the Holy Kinship, showing the adult Mary sitting, rather awkwardly, in her mother's lap.

On the other hand, the Dominicans, following the teaching of Thomas Aquinas and Albertus Magnus, sponsored images of Mary nursing Jesus. Mary's milk, derived—as the scholarly Dominicans believed—from her purified blood, reminded viewers that Mary, like all humans, needed Christ's redemption from original sin, even though Dominicans had no doubts that when Jesus was conceived, Mary bore no original sin. Intellectually, the image of the nursing virgin was also typical of the humanistic climate of the Renaissance, reminding viewers of Jesus's shared humanity. Ordinary women prayed before images of the nursing Virgin, asking for abundant breast milk and a healthy child. Relics of Mary's milk reassured devotees of her corporeal reality while providing miraculous healing, the goal of pilgrims in shrines all over Europe. Northern Europe's leading Marian pilgrimage shrine was in England at 'Mary's house' in Walsingham, with its famous phial of Mary's breastmilk.

Well after Bernard of Clairvaux's lifetime and on into the 17th century a famous legend, the *Lactation of St Bernard* (Figure 15), linked him with the Virgin's milk. As Bernard in a moment of doubt was praying before an image of the nursing Virgin, the statue came to life. Mary quelled Bernard's doubts by squeezing three drops of breast milk onto his lips and assuring him of her zealous intercession with the son she was nursing. This story illustrates the popular belief that the Virgin's aid was most readily secured in the presence of her statue or image. Not surprisingly, then, in medieval Spanish churches statues of the Virgin outnumbered crucifixes. There was only one Jesus, but Mary had many manifestations.

By the late 15th century Europe balanced on the cusp of the Enlightenment. Rationalist thinking, scientific enquiry, and, not

15. *Lactation of St Bernard*, engraving, *c.*1485, Master IAM of Zwolle.

least, the invention of the printing press were changing the way Europeans saw themselves and their world, and the Church faced unprecedented challenges. Among these were questions about the proper place of the Virgin in Christian doctrine and devotion.

Chapter 7
Modern Mary—Reformation to the present

Protestant Reformation—Catholic Reformation

On 31 October 1517, an Augustinian priest named Martin Luther reportedly nailed his *95 Theses* to the door of Wittenberg Cathedral in Germany. Protesting the Church's practice of selling indulgences, Luther set a match to already smouldering controversies that would soon divide European Christians into Catholics and Protestants. Luther did not intend to break up the western Church. With other devout Christians of his time he shared the conviction that church reform was needed, particularly with regard to indulgences; this was a church practice which allowed people to reduce the number of years they or loved ones spent in Purgatory by performing good works, pilgrimage, and prayer, but also, in Luther's time, by paying cash. The Virgin Mary was not on Luther's mind. In the *95 Theses* Mary comes up just once, for rhetorical effect: 'To consider papal indulgences so great that they could absolve a man even if he had...violated the mother of God is madness.'

However, the refusal of church authorities to address Luther's critique of church governance and doctrine—he was excommunicated—drew together like-minded theologians and European princes first in opposition and then to a full break with Rome and papal authority. In response, the 'Roman' Catholic

Church embarked on its own reform with the Council of Trent (1545–63). Council delegates clarified Catholic faith and doctrine while reaffirming Catholicism's doctrinal basis in both scripture (the Bible) and church tradition. In this endeavour, Marian devotion was promoted as a unifying force.

This chapter looks at the Virgin Mary from the 16th century to the present. The period witnessed momentous events, beginning with the Protestant Reformation, but with regard to the Virgin Mary it was characterized by the push and pull of religious ideals as clerical and lay Christians grappled not only with the rationalist and individualistic ideals of the Enlightenment but the expanding global reach of the Church. At Trent, church leaders formulated an intellectual text-based code of religious practice for all Catholics to follow, whether in Europe, the New World, Asia, or Africa. For the next 400 years, Catholicism was 'Tridentine' (maintaining the ideology of Trent), substantially changing only with the reforms of the Second Vatican Council ('Vatican II') in the early 1960s.

By the late 18th century, the spirit of enquiry and debate that had energized the Trent reformers receded before the threat of European revolutionary movements that sought to eliminate the influence of the Catholic Church in government and society. Coinciding with the so-called 'Marian Century'—from Pius IX's declaration in 1854 of the Immaculate Conception to 1950 when Mary's Assumption became dogma under Pius XII—came Vatican resistance to rational secularism, most famously represented by Pius IX's *Syllabus of Errors* (1864). This document denounced as 'errors' such secular values as 'Human reason, without any reference whatsoever to God', separation of Church and state, and religious freedom. The Marian Century effectively ended when Vatican II, in what John XXIII described as *aggiornamento* or 'bringing up to date', shifted away from the anti-intellectual retrenchment represented by the *Syllabus of Errors* to uphold the compatibility of faith and reason, religious toleration, lay engagement in the Church, and a renewed commitment to both scripture and Christ-centred Marian veneration.

Protestants and Mary

The Protestant Reformation of the 16th century was itself a reflex of Europe's new embrace of reason. The scientific revolution was challenging previously unquestioned beliefs grounded in divine revelation, most crucially the Bible and church teaching. Like the internet today, the printing press democratized access to knowledge. Printing stimulated democratic thinking and consequent challenges to established authority that led at their most dramatic to the American and French Revolutions. Perhaps most radical of all, people began to compartmentalize their lives into the separate secular and religious domains characteristic of modern western society. Adding to this ferment of ideas was the European encounter with the New World which tested European assumptions about humanity itself. Attempts to subjugate indigenous peoples were soon followed by expanded trade in human bodies—enslaved people—from Africa to supplement the labour of indigenous workers killed by European-borne diseases. All these factors affected attitudes toward and beliefs about the Virgin Mary.

For many Protestants, veneration of the Virgin clashed with their insistence that doctrine and practice be based only on the Bible. They found no scriptural justification for Mary's perpetual virginity or intercession and, citing the Ten Commandments, many Reformers demanded an end to 'idol worship' by removing sacred images from churches and homes. The Virgin Mary became the lightning rod for Protestant polemics both physical—widespread destruction of Marian images—and rhetorical, as reformers ridiculed images of the Virgin, mocked Marian relics, and disparaged many of her miracles as immoral. The sizeable indulgences pilgrims earned at Marian shrines and churches prompted Protestants to reject pilgrimages in general. The Reformation all but erased Mary from Protestant spirituality.

Only at Christmas did Mary figure in liturgy, pageants, carols, or hymns, such as the 'Virgin Mary's Song' (1707) by English minister Isaac Watts. Based appropriately on a biblical text—Luke's *Magnificat*—it concludes with a sober Protestant admonition:

> Let every nation call her bless'd,
> And endless years prolong her fame;
> But God alone must be ador'd;
> Holy and reverend is his name.

Nevertheless, Mary's disappearance from the Protestant world was neither instantaneous nor total. No unified Protestant stance on Marian devotion was ever formulated. Lutherans kept three Marian feasts—the Annunciation, Visitation, and Purification. And it took time for Protestant preachers to reorient worshippers to new interpretations of scripture. In his 1555 Harmony of the Gospel, John Calvin wrote that Gabriel's greeting, 'Hail Mary, full of grace', proved that the Virgin 'deserves to be called blessed, for God has accorded her a singular distinction, to prepare His Son for the world'. By singing the *Magnificat*, Luther taught, Mary showed Christians how to pray with humility. One of Protestant Johann Sebastian Bach's most beloved works is his 1723 choral setting of Mary's *Magnificat*—in Latin. Although Marian intercession was denied because it implied Jesus was subservient to his mother, Mary's humility, obedience, and faith provided the quintessential model for Protestant piety. Mary was still idealized as a woman and mother, albeit a silent and obedient one. Luther himself was tolerant of images, which could still be found in private homes and even in some Reformed churches. In Nuremberg, Germany, forty *Hausmadonnen*, Mary images on house exteriors, survived into the 19th century.

Roman Catholics and the Council of Trent

The Catholic reformers of Trent reaffirmed Mary's perpetual virginity, intercession, pilgrimage, and relics, but the Virgin Mary who emerged from Trent was also shaped by some of the same misgivings that Protestants had voiced about the cult of Mary. Catholic reformers insisted on doctrinal and ritual uniformity with a Christ-centric emphasis over against local or regional Marian practices, many of which the councillors at Trent considered superstitious and theologically suspect. Pius V stressed that the words and ritual gestures in Trent's revised *Roman Missal* of 1570 were based on careful study of 'works of ancient and approved authors concerning the...sacred rites'. The goal of a standardized liturgy is clear in the Pope's directive that the *Missal* be printed so that 'priests would know what prayers to use and what rites and ceremonies they are to observe from now on'.

A more dignified Virgin replaced the comparatively free-wheeling and assertive Mary of the medieval–Renaissance miracle tales and mystery plays, the Mary who attracted so much Protestant derision. New artistic standards of dignity and decorum effectively erased Mary's relation to physical motherhood. Gone were portrayals of the infant Mary in her mother's womb, Byzantine-style Nativities with Mary reclining on a birth couch, pregnant Virgins, and Holy Kinship scenes. Nursing Virgins disappeared, the casualty of Protestant ridicule and Trent's spiritualization of Mary. Even the naked infant Jesus became offensive. In his *Treatise on Sacred Images* (1570), Johannes Molanus complained, 'It is well known that artists often paint or sculpt the infant Jesus naked;...what sort of edification can there be in this nakedness?'

Mary often appeared without her son in post-Tridentine art, especially in images of the Immaculate Conception. Advocates of the Immaculate Conception made headway at Trent, but ultimately the council sidestepped a formal declaration acclaiming Mary only as the 'blessed and immaculate Virgin'. Catholic guidelines for depicting the Immaculate Conception drew upon the Bible, especially Revelation 12. According to Francisco Pacheco's Church-approved *Arte de la Pintura* of 1649, the Virgin Immaculate was to be a beautiful young girl, twelve or thirteen years old...She should be painted wearing a white tunic and a blue mantle. She is surrounded by the sun...which sweetly blends into the sky. Rays of light emanate from her head, around which is a ring of twelve stars...Under her feet is the moon.

These guidelines added a new dimension to a familiar late medieval image—the Virgin of Guadalupe is an example—already prized for its association with substantial papal indulgences.

In Bartolomé Murillo's *Immaculate Conception of El Escorial* (1678) (Figure 16) a pre-pubescent Virgin floats amidst glowing clouds while four naked *putti* (genderless baby angels) offer plants symbolic of the Immaculate Conception: lily, rose, palm, and olive. Suspended in heaven, untethered from time, this Mary also reflected a belief rooted in God's plan of salvation articulated by Franciscan Lawrence of Brindisi: Mary 'was the predestined Mother of Christ, having been predestined before all creatures, together with Christ, the firstborn of every creature'. Mary the 'Gate of Heaven' was conceived before creation in the mind of God. The epitome of ethereal purity, Mary is poised above—rather than of—the earth. Mary of the *Miraculous Medal* (Figure 1, Chapter 1) and the often saccharine 19th- and 20th-century portrayals of Mary are direct heirs of this visual tradition.

At the Council of Trent in 1563 marriage became one of the Seven Sacraments, although the council still judged it holier to 'remain in virginity or celibacy than to be joined in marriage'. Prior to Trent, marriage had been a family and civil matter, although, as is evident in paintings of the 'Marriage of the Virgin', couples could receive a priest's blessing in front of—not inside—a church. The marriage of Mary and Joseph was now held up as the ideal marriage in the service of God with a reminder that the holy couple practised perfect chastity. Images of the Holy Family joined

16. *Immaculate Conception of El Escorial*, 1678, Bartolomé Esteban
Murillo, Prado Museum, Madrid, Spain.

the repertory of approved Catholic art, and Joseph, a formerly marginal figure as Jesus's foster-father, gained new distinction as head of the family. In place of the traditional elderly Joseph hunched on the sidelines in Nativity scenes, now a younger, manlier Joseph kept watch over mother and child. Views expressed by theologian Joseph Gerson in the 15th century now aligned with the Tridentine Church's patriarchal principles that, as the perfect woman, Mary would have submitted to her husband's authority.

Still, the Tridentine Mary was by no means always passive and non-corporeal. In certain contexts, Mary's warrior persona persisted. Mary was credited in 1571 for the unexpected naval victory by an undermanned Catholic Holy League over the Muslim Ottoman fleet at Lepanto. Pius V affirmed that while the battle against the Infidel raged off the coast of Greece, the victory had been won because simultaneously in Rome Mary's Rosary Confraternity, a lay association, had been praying the rosary. In honour of Lepanto, Pius V established the feast day of Our Lady of Victory; in 1571 Gregory XIII changed the name to the Feast of the Holy Rosary. Images of Our Lady of the Rosary and Our Lady of Victory, especially in prints, often incorporated triumphant motifs such as Mary and the infant Jesus impaling Muslims or Protestants with a cross (Figure 17).

Persecuted Catholics in Protestant England recited the rosary fortified by the promise in Jesuit Henry Garnet's *Societie of the Rosary* that the Virgin 'mightily overcometh' her own and 'her devout clients'' adversaries'. The 20th-century Cold War engendered a similar phenomenon when the Virgin Mary fought against 'godless Communists', routinely designated as the modern-day Antichrist. In the mid-1940s a hitherto obscure 1917 apparition of the Virgin in Fátima, Portugal, gained prominence as Catholics were urged to heed the Virgin of Fátima's command to 'pray the Rosary for the conversion of Russia'.

17. *Virgin and Christ Triumphing over the Heretics*, engraving, 1598, Antonius Wierix. A rosary labelled 'VICTRIX' (female victor) encircles Mary and Jesus. The cross impales a pile of defeated Protestants holding their Bibles. In the lower portion of the print the biblical heroine, Jael, foreshadows the Virgin's victory by pounding a tent peg into the head of Sisera, the enemy general (Judges 4–5).

Global Mary

Inasmuch as Christianity reached Ethiopia, India, and China in its early centuries, the Virgin has always been global. In the 16th century the Virgin accompanied the forces of Spain, Portugal, and France in their conquests, missions, and colonies in the New World and Asia. However, cultural influence worked in two directions, and perceptions of the Virgin were inevitably affected by the non-European peoples to whom she was introduced. Jesuits in Japan no less than the Augustinians, Franciscans, and

Dominicans who evangelized the New World were willing at times to adapt Catholic doctrine to indigenous traditions. Many made the effort to learn about the beliefs of their intended converts. For their part, the peoples they tried to convert were not passive subjects and they actively negotiated between their old and new religious traditions.

Portuguese Jesuit missionaries brought Christianity to Japan in the 1540s, but after 1630 the expulsion of missionaries and proscription of Christianity forced Japanese Christians to worship secretly. One survival strategy was to disguise Christian images in Buddhist form. The Virgin Mary was venerated through figures of the Son-Bringing Kannon (Figure 18), the feminized bodhisattva of compassion, portrayed as a mother holding a son. Like Mary, Kannon played an intercessory role in Japanese Pure Land Buddhism and was associated with transformation and miracles. The meditation practice of repetitive rosary prayers also harmonized easily with numerically formulated Pure Land prayer cycles.

Jesuit missionaries could evangelize in Japan only as long as Japanese rulers protected them. Power relations were different in the New World where Mary—sometimes entitled *La Conquistadora*—arrived as patroness of the *Conquistadores*. In New Spain, Mary's presence was so conspicuous among the early conquerors that at first local peoples believed the name of God and all Christian images was Mary. Nevertheless, as in the case of Mexico's Virgin of Guadalupe (see Chapter 4), indigenous traditions and European Marian traditions mingled in complex ways.

Mary entered Mexico in 1519 with the Spanish conquerors, many of whom were devoted to the Castilian black Virgin of Guadalupe, a town in Estremadura. The Virgin of Guadalupe occupied Spain's wealthiest and most politically connected shrine and had been closely associated with the *Reconquista*, Christian Spain's

18. *Virgin Mary as the Son-Bringing Kannon*, Dehua Porcelain, 17th century. Nantoyōsō Collection, Japan.

centuries-long struggle to expel the Muslims, which Spain finally achieved in 1492. Since the 13th century, Spain had looked to Mary both as symbol and leader in its struggle against Islam. Victorious Spaniards regularly transformed mosques into churches dedicated to the Virgin. The expulsion of the Muslims in

1492 was such a living memory among the *Conquistadores* that, at first, they identified Aztec temples as mosques.

Such was the prestige of the Spanish Virgin of Guadalupe among the colonial rulers of Mexico that when the Virgin appeared to the Nahua Juan Diego, the apparitional Mary's appeal among the growing Creole communities (people of pure Spanish descent but born in the New World) was enhanced by identifying her with the powerful Spanish Virgin. Yet the Mexican Virgin of Guadalupe (see Figure 9, Chapter 4) bears little resemblance to the diminutive medieval Black Madonna still revered in Guadalupe, Spain, today and who belongs to the same Throne of Wisdom statue-type as the Virgin of Montserrat (see Figure 8, Chapter 4). Instead, Mexico's *La Morenita* reflects the newer Immaculate Conception iconography which was familiar in colonial Mexico from imported prints and works created by indigenous artists in art schools that missionaries had established.

Some idea of the complex history of Marian traditions among indigenous Americans and the colonizing Spanish may be perceived in the *Nueva Corónica* of 1615 by the Inca (Quechua) noble and convert Felipe Guaman Poma. The *Corónica* included Poma's drawing of a crowned and martial Virgin pitching snow and sand from her heavenly perch atop an angel 'onto the eyes of the infidel Indians' to repel an Inca siege from the city of Cuzco. Poma wrote his history of the Andes to inform Philip II of Spain about Spanish injustices in Peru, and he addressed the Spanish king as a fellow-aristocrat. As an assimilated Inca convert, however, Poma occupied a precarious position vis-à-vis the colonial authorities. Thus, he described the Inca defeat at Cuzco as Mary's blessing, bringing Christianity to the Inca. Nevertheless, it was not long before the Virgin had absorbed aspects of the Inca deity *Pachamama*, portrayed as the Virgin of Cerro Rico in the form of a triangular mountain bedecked in Andean flora and fauna but with a female face and hands.

Vernacular Catholicism: the rosary and apparitions of the Virgin

The Trent reformers expounded doctrinal and institutional issues to unify the Church, but theirs was an elite literary enterprise. The role of lay Catholics within the Church was largely ignored even as the reformers intended all Catholics to be doctrinally informed and to lay aside what were considered superstitious practices. While gaps had always existed between official and popular practice, in the centuries after the Council of Trent the official guardians of Catholic doctrine repeatedly found themselves adjusting, accommodating, or incorporating what Catholic historian Nathan Mitchell calls Catholic 'vernacular religion'. This broad term encompasses local folk traditions, the beliefs of the poor, and the reflections of elite humanist Catholic scholars in addition to the ecstatic visions of Catholic mystics and Marian apparitions to humble witnesses. Two well-known features of Catholicism illustrate the give-and-take of vernacular and official Catholicism across the globe: the rosary and apparitions of the Virgin.

The rosary

A rosary is at once a crown, a set of mantra-like meditative prayers, and a string of beads-plus-crucifix used to keep count of the prayers. According to medieval tradition, each Hail Mary—the Virgin's favourite prayer—generated a rose; by reciting multiple Hail Marys a devotee wove a crown of roses for the delight of heaven's supreme intercessor. Pious legend describes the Virgin personally presenting the first rosary to St Dominic in the 13th century, but rosary use only began to flourish in the 15th century and was one of several techniques for reciting multiple prayers in honour of Jesus or Mary. In 1569 Pius V standardized the 59-bead rosary and the 150 Hail Marys (see Box 2) to be recited while

> **Box 2 Hail Mary Prayer, revised Roman Breviary, 1568**
>
> Hail Mary, full of Grace, Blessed art thou among women
> and blessed be the fruit of thy womb, Jesus.
> Holy Mary, Mother of God, pray for us sinners,
> now and at the hour of our death, Amen.

contemplating the Mysteries of the Rosary: fifteen events from the life of Mary and Jesus arranged in three sets of five, culminating with the Assumption and Coronation of the Virgin. This rosary practice remained unchanged until 2002 when John Paul II added five additional 'Luminous' Mysteries.

Initially, many church officials had misgivings about the rosary because of its use by lay women and men, often in confraternities without priestly supervision. Yet by linking the rosary with the victory at Lepanto the Pope helped bring a popular practice into the framework of official Catholicism. The rosary also connected lay Catholics with the Eucharist. At the time, lay Eucharistic participation consisted of receiving the communion wafer in a ritual conducted in incomprehensible and often inaudible Latin. By saying the rosary during Mass, worshippers enjoyed ritual agency in a parallel Eucharist of their own words and gestures. As a material thing which the worshipper could touch and hold, the rosary provided a bodily link to the Virgin's spiritual sustenance.

Rosary use spread quickly across the Catholic world, helped along by easily transported and popular rosary prints (see Figure 17). The global dimensions of the rosary come across in one of Inca Guaman Poma's *Coronica* drawings in which a devout Christian couple of African descent pray the rosary before an image of Mary the Immaculate Conception, at the time the most popular type of Virgin in the New World (Figure 19). Guaman Poma acclaimed the benefits of Christianity for everyone in colonial Peru, including the offspring of enslaved Africans whose European attire and evident devotion to the Virgin are meant to signal their uplifted and civilized character.

Among Protestants, in contrast, the rosary was so emblematic of Catholicism that England in the 16th century outlawed rosary beads; owning a rosary in anti-Catholic England could mean

19. 'Africans [labelled 'Guineans'] brought to the New World [Peru] pray the rosary to the Virgin,' manuscript drawing, Felipe Guaman Poma, *El Primer Nueva Corónica y Buen Gobierno* (*The First New Chronicle and Good Government*), 1615. Royal Library, Copenhagen, Denmark.

forfeiture of lands and goods. For many English Catholics with rare access to priests, the rosary, especially when recited in the company of a few others, could also function as an alternative Eucharist. English Catholics were encouraged to join the continental Dominican Society of the Rosary which allowed them to earn indulgences via the rosary even if they could not celebrate the Eucharist. In America, Protestants viewed the rosary with the same distaste they felt for what they believed to be Catholic Mariolatry, but for Catholic immigrants to America, rosary devotions at once connected them with the communities they had left behind and reinforced communal and spiritual solidarity under the wing of the Virgin, a source of comfort in their often-inhospitable new country.

In the 1960s when the vernacular Mass was introduced, the rosary's Eucharistic role diminished. As the Vatican II Church called worshipers to a renewed Eucharistic devotion to Jesus, the Marian focus of the rosary prayer ritual was deemed inappropriate during Mass. The Vatican II Church's call for doctrinal engagement with the Bible also displaced Marian devotions, and popular features of Marian piety such as scapulars and novenas began to disappear. Symbols of Catholic solidarity like the rosary and Marian devotion also grew less relevant to the younger generation of white northern Europeans as well as American Catholics who had assimilated into mainstream middle-class politics and culture. In many developed nations today, the rosary tends to be associated with conservative Catholicism. On the other hand, it remains popular across the broad spectrum of southern European, Latinx, and other global Catholics.

Apparitions

Apparitions of holy beings have been reported throughout Christian history, but each event has its own specific cultural and historical context. Currently the Vatican has no office dedicated to apparitions, Marian or otherwise. The local bishop is expected to investigate and rule on its merits, and no Catholic is required to accept the truth of any Marian apparition. Since Vatican II, the Church has most often remained neutral, insisting that the most important aspect of an apparition is not empirical proof but that it inspires greater Christian charity. When Vatican authorities finally approved pilgrimage to the Medjugorje apparition shrine in 2019, they also maintained their earlier ruling on Mary's apparition that 'it is undetermined at this time if it is of supernatural origin'. Nevertheless, because official parish or diocesan pilgrimage is only permitted to Vatican-approved shrines, approval has serious ramifications for spiritual prestige, not to mention shrine income.

Today, the best-known Marian apparition sites are Guadalupe in Mexico (1531), La Salette (1846) and Lourdes (1858) in France, Knock in Ireland (1879), Fátima in Portugal (1917), Beauraing in Belgium (1932), and Medjugorje in Bosnia-Herzegovina (since 1981). However, these places are the exceptions. Most apparition sites never achieve long-lasting and international renown, fading quickly or retaining only a local following. When she appears, Mary seems to favour communities with a long tradition of interaction with spirits in local caves, trees, and springs. Apparitions have also typically taken place in times of social stresses and in marginalized communities that resent wealthier towns and villages in their region. In the early 1980s, when socio-economic pressures exacerbated tensions between Orthodox Serbs, Muslim Bosnians, and Catholic Croatians, the Virgin's appearance in ethnically Croatian Medjugorje was hailed by Croatians as evidence of their unique chosenness.

In the past two centuries, Mary's visionaries have usually been young, female, impoverished, uneducated, frequently ill, and even subject to domestic violence, like Bernadette Soubirous, the 14-year-old seer of Lourdes. As an apparition site gains respect and develops an official story, the visionary's youth comes to be interpreted, like Mary's, as a sign of innocence and purity. Young seers are often subject to repeated interrogation by various authorities, and while the official shrine narrative insists visionaries never altered their story, archival evidence complicates this claim. In apparition stories, the seer usually describes a glowing figure or woman—not always at first identified as the Virgin—who communicates in the local language. Juan Diego heard the Virgin speaking in Quechua, for example. At Lourdes, when religious authorities instructed Bernadette to ask the name of the being she called *Aquéro* (local dialect, 'that'), the Lady's answer was, 'I am the Immaculate Conception.' As this occurred only four years after Pius IX's highly controversial declaration of the doctrine of the Immaculate Conception, the publicity around Bernadette's visions at Lourdes reinforced both the Church's agenda and the authenticity of the Lourdes shrine.

In an apparition the Virgin may request the repair or construction of a chapel or comment on a local priest's behaviour; she may warn that lax local religious attitudes have drawn God's ire that can only be averted if the community returns to the rosary and attendance at Mass; she may call for world peace, as she did at Fátima in 1917 during the First World War. Since the end of the 20th century the Virgin's message has grown more apocalyptic, with warnings about end-time calamities, and the visionaries are sometimes middle-class women and men. The apparition narratives as promoted by the leading Marian shrines take time to evolve. The official narrative and shrine managers largely adhere to a conservative Catholic religious and political agenda that demands ritual orthodoxy, traditional piety, and allegiance to Rome. The apparitional Virgin does not critique patriarchal power structures; she does not call for social transformation or the ordination of women.

Such generalizations, however, must be weighed alongside the complicated origin history of each Marian shrine as well as its unique historical trajectory. The phenomenal success of Lourdes in the 19th century was indeed due to church and business interests supported by conservative French newspapers that promoted a pro-monarchist/anti-republican ideology steeped in Marian piety. But Lourdes also flourished thanks to a determined group of devout women who insisted—in the face of ridicule from France's influential medical establishment—on the Virgin's power to effect miraculous cures. Twenty-first-century pilgrims to Lourdes encounter not monarchists but a lived version of an alternative society reminiscent of Mary's *Magnificat* where the sick and disabled are empowered and the able-bodied feel privileged to serve.

The Virgin of Guadalupe's significance has also evolved. Miguel Sánchez's 1648 *Imagen de la Virgen Maria*, the earliest account of the apparition, hailed her as 'Assistant Conqueror' by whose aid the 'heathenism of the New World was conquered'. Late 20th-century pilgrims to Mexico City's Guadalupe shrine included conservative Catholics but also, famously, the lesbian *muherista* Gloria Anzaldúa. Catholic liberation theologians such as Virgilio Elizondo celebrated the Virgin of Guadalupe's indigenous roots and her power to overcome the negative effects of conquest and colonization on the people of Mexico. California Farm Labor Union activists in the 1960s marched with banners of Guadalupe and inspired Chicana artist Ester Hernandez's 1975 poster of the Virgin of Guadalupe performing a karate kick in defence of the 'rights of Chicanos' (Figure 20).

As a general rule, apparitions are initially greeted with scepticism by local church authorities and their superiors, not least because of the marginal social status or problematic loyalties of the visionaries. Bernadette seemed too abject a girl to merit a personal visit from the Virgin. At Medjugorje, the local bishop and proponents of the apparitions engaged in a jurisdictional dispute between Croatian Franciscans and the Vatican. Marian apparitions are essentially upwellings of local energy and agency; if Mary is communicating directly with ordinary, even lower-class lay people, the Church's claim to be the sole mediator between

20. *La Vergen de Guadalupe Defendienda los Derechos de los Xicanos*
(The Virgin of Guadalupe defends the Rights of Chicanos), etching,
Ester Hernandez, 1975.

God and faithful Catholics is challenged. In the case of successful
apparition sites, the inevitable Church–local power struggle
over an apparition has by and large resulted in a mutual
accommodation that acknowledges church authority and orthodox
theology while sustaining local pride, prestige, and distinctiveness.

Whither Mary? Vatican II and after

At the Second Vatican Council, one faction of bishops demanded greater honours for Jesus's mother, including Co-Redeemer status with Christ; the other faction worried that Marian devotion had exceeded the bounds of Catholic doctrine and was distracting the faithful from recognizing the Eucharist as the 'source and summit' of Christian faith. Furthermore, many Vatican II delegates sought open dialogue with Protestants and encouraged a new focus on Mary's biblical aspects with which Protestants could agree. The Council's final pronouncement, *Lumen Gentium* (1964), reflects the view of the bishops who called for Marian restraint. It praises Mary Queen of the Universe while cautioning that 'no creature could be counted as equal with the Incarnate Word and Redeemer'; Mary's intercessory role 'flows forth from the superabundance of the merits of Christ...and draws all its power from it'.

In the late 1950s and 1960s an influential movement in Catholicism known as liberation theology arose in South America. Liberation theology was informed by Marxism as well as the American civil rights movement and, eventually, feminism. Protesting widespread poverty and social injustice, liberation theologians like Dominican Gustavo Gutiérrez in Peru preached God's preferential option for the poor, demanding justice for the poor and oppressed in this world, not just in the world to come. One of liberation theology's key texts is Mary's *Magnificat*, which describes a God 'who has brought down the powerful from their thrones and lifted up the lowly' (Luke 1:52). Liberation theologians taught that Mary, as a peasant *madre soltera* (Spanish, 'mother on her own') whose son was executed by an unjust state, was the sister of the poor, sharing their struggles and modelling a fierce faith in the face of injustice. In turn, feminist Mariology celebrates Mary for her fortitude and for her active choice, in bearing Jesus, to participate in God's plan for human liberation. Mary thus becomes a model not just for modern Catholic women but for an inclusive Church. Nevertheless, progressive Catholic movements like liberation theology have experienced limited global success in the 21st century.

How the Virgin Mary will fare as the 21st century advances is an open question. Broadly speaking, the Catholic Church finds itself no less polarized than the rest of society. Faithful progressive Catholics advocate social justice and lay empowerment; they welcome LGBTQ persons and call for married priests and the ordination of women. Liberation theology's Mary *madre soltera* offers an empowering model of inclusive faith-seeking justice, but among this group of Catholics private devotion to Mary has diminished. For their part, traditionalist Catholics yearn for pre-Vatican II Marian piety which offers them the security of time-honoured tradition. Traditionalists oppose progressive social issues, married priests, and the ordination of women while endorsing a strong clerical hierarchy. Yet many Catholics today blame this same hierarchical structure for enabling both worldwide clergy sex abuse and its cover-up. Numerous Catholics have left behind a Church they felt had betrayed them. The Virgin Mary, meanwhile, remains untainted by any association with the scandal, and many former Catholics admit they still pray to the Virgin.

There is another global phenomenon that threatens the future of Marian piety; increasing numbers of Hispanic, African, and Asian Catholics are converting to Evangelical Protestantism. Evangelical missionaries preach against Marian piety, although not usually to the extent of publicly insulting and vandalizing a statue of Brazil's Catholic patroness, the Black Virgin of Aparecido, as a Protestant minister did on national television in 1995.

In the digital 21st century, despite the many Marian websites, it appears that online involvement in Marian spirituality remains a fringe phenomenon. In the last few years some Episcopal and Lutheran churches in the United States calling for solidarity with immigrants from the global South have begun to celebrate the festival of Our Lady of Guadalupe, but they are exceptions in mainstream Protestantism. Traditionally, Marian devotion has flourished where devotees hope for a personal encounter with the Blessed Mother. This explains the ongoing attraction of the leading Marian pilgrimage shines—Lourdes, Medjugorje, and above all, Guadalupe—where the number of pilgrims continues to grow each year.

A fascinating aspect of Mexico's shrine of Guadalupe, the most popular pilgrimage site, however, is that while many of the pilgrims fall firmly into the traditional Catholic camp, a great many other pilgrims to *La Morenita*, especially women, give little credence to the magisterium (teaching authority) of the Catholic Church. Many identify as New Age-inspired devotees of some form of 'Great Mother'. Feminists, Queers, and Latinx come to the shrine of Guadalupe assured of the Virgin's welcome, solace, and support when other religious spaces have closed their doors to them. Pilgrimage may be a famously Catholic practice, nurtured and enhanced by Tridentine Catholicism, but pilgrimage is also a timeless religious phenomenon. Pilgrims have always enjoyed *communitas*, the egalitarian fellow-feeling which welcomes everyone encountered along the way and which disinclines pilgrims to worry overmuch about doctrinal purity. Perhaps in our global world, this spiritually inclusive character of pilgrimage to Guadalupe offers a model for both Marian devotion and a better world.

Timeline

0 BCE/CE	Birth of Jesus (traditional date)
c.30 CE	Crucifixion of Jesus by Romans
c.50–7	Paul's letters (in New Testament)
c.70	Gospel of Mark
c.80	Gospel of Matthew
c.90	Gospel of Luke
c.100	Gospel of John
c.120	New Testament books completed
c.145	*Protevangelium of James*
311	Edict of Toleration issued by Roman Tetrarchs Galerius, Constantine, and Licinius legalizes Christianity, ends persecution of Christians
325	Nicene Creed (emended 381 to include Mary)
431	Council of Ephesus agrees Mary may be called *Theotokos*
622	Islam established by Muhammad in Arabia
1054	'Great Schism'—split between Orthodox (eastern) and Catholic (western) Churches
1453	Fall of the Byzantine (Orthodox Christian) Empire to Muslim Ottoman Turks
1517	Protestant Reformation begins

1531	Apparition of Mary to Aztec Juan Diego (Mexican Lady of Guadalupe)
1545–63	Council of Trent defines Catholic doctrines and practices in response to Protestant Reformation
1789	French Revolution; anti-clerical (i.e. anti-Catholic) legislation in France in favour of strict governmental secularism
1854	Pope Pius IX defines the Immaculate Conception in the encyclical, *Ineffabilis Deus*
1858	Apparition of Mary to Bernadette Soubirous, Lourdes, France
1950	Pope Pius XII defines the Assumption of the Virgin Mary in the encyclical *Munificentissimus Deus*
1962–5	Second Vatican Council ('Vatican II') legislates modernizing reforms in *Lumen Gentium*, the Dogmatic Constitution on the Church

Glossary

Akathistos (Greek, 'not sitting') renowned Orthodox (s.v.) hymn to the Mother of God sung while standing; composed in the 7th century.

Annunciation ordinarily the event wherein the Angel Gabriel announces to Mary the conception of Jesus (Luke 1:26–38).

Apocrypha Jewish and Christian texts written roughly between the 2nd century BCE and the 4th century CE that were often influential but not recognized as canonical (s.v.).

Assumption Mary's elevation in body and soul into heaven at the end of her life; *see also* 'Dormition'.

canonical religious text accepted as authoritative.

Christology branch of theology that focuses on the identity and nature of Christ.

Coptic ethnic Christian communities in Egypt; also their religious language.

Council of Ephesus church council in 431 on the coast of Asia Minor; reached a consensus to call the Virgin Mary '*Theotokos*' (s.v.); first ecumenical articulation of Mary's role in Christian theology.

Council of Trent Roman Catholic council (1545–63) that, in light of the Protestant crisis, reaffirmed and revitalized traditional Catholic beliefs about Mary, the Eucharist, relics, etc.; its teachings defined the principles of the Catholic Reformation.

Docetism from the Greek verb 'to seem', the belief, considered a Christian heresy, that Jesus only 'seemed' human while in reality being fully divine.

dogma officially mandated belief.

Dormition (Latin, 'falling asleep') the end of Mary's life and her subsequent fate; *see also* 'Assumption'.

Epiphany (Greek, 'appearance', i.e. of Jesus in the world) the visit of the Magi/Wise Men to the infant Jesus (Matthew 2:1–12).

Gentile Jewish term for anyone not Jewish.

Gentile Christian non-Jewish convert to Christianity.

Gnosticism strand of early Christian beliefs that, while diverse, generally claimed the world was created by a flawed god; Jesus was sent from heaven to reveal this to humans and give them knowledge (Greek, *gnosis*) to escape the created world and to reunite with the true and eternal 'One'.

heterodox types of Christianity judged 'unorthodox', i.e. not conforming to correct Christian doctrine (*see* orthodox).

homily sermon.

Hypostatic Union theological term referring to Christ's co-existing human and divine natures.

Immaculate Conception Catholic dogma (s.v.) proclaimed in 1854 that Mary was conceived free from original sin in her mother's womb. (Often confused with Mary's virginal conception of Jesus.)

liturgy rules for worship and/or words used in worship.

Magnificat Mary's song of joy in Luke 1:46–55; named for the first word in the Latin version meaning '[my soul] magnifies [the Lord]'; Orthodox name 'Ode of the *Theotokos*'.

Marian having to do with the Virgin Mary.

Nicene Creed first church-wide summation of Christian belief, formulated at Nicaea in 325 CE.

original sin disobedience of Adam and Eve in the Garden of Eden (Genesis 3) that alienated humans from God; Christians believe Jesus's death and resurrection remedied this by freeing them from original sin and granting eternal life.

Orthodox (upper case) one of the three large Christian denominations; concentrated in Greece, Russia, Cyprus, Eastern Europe, the Middle East, Ethiopia.

orthodox (lower case) accepted Christian belief, in contrast to heterodox (s.v.) and 'heretical', which is unacceptable or wrong belief.

Panagia (Greek, 'All Holy') Greek Orthodox title for the Mother of Jesus.

Pentecost Christian festival fifty days after Easter; commemorates the descent of the Holy Spirit on Jesus's disciples (Acts 2).

perpetual virginity/*Virginitas in partu/Virginitas post partum* applies to the extent of the Virgin Mary's virginity; *in partu* giving birth; *post partum*: after giving birth.

Protestant *see* Reformation.

Reformation western European Christian movement, traditionally said to begin in 1517 with Martin Luther, who called for reform of certain church doctrines and practices; divided western Christianity into Protestants (those who protested perceived wrongdoing in the Church) and Roman Catholics (those who remained loyal to the papacy and Vatican-approved teaching and practice).

Roman Catholic *see* Reformation; Council of Trent.

rosary set of repeated prayers addressed to the Virgin Mary by Catholics consisting of the Hail Mary, the Our Father, and other prayers; also, string of beads-plus-crucifix used to keep track of the prayers.

supersessionism Christian view that the coming of Jesus the Messiah renders Judaism null and void (now rejected by many, but not all, Christian denominations).

Theotokos (Greek, 'One Who Gives Birth to God') Marian (s.v.) title associated with the Council of Ephesus (s.v.) in 431 acknowledging Mary's role in Christianity as the Mother of God.

Trent *see* Council of Trent; Tridentine.

Tridentine doctrine and practices endorsed or inspired by the Council of Trent (s.v.) that characterized Catholic Christianity from 1563 until the Second Vatican Council of 1962–5.

Vatican II Second Vatican Council, 1962–5, called by Pope John XXIII for the renewal of the Catholic Church. Modernizing decisions included: vernacular Mass, greater involvement of lay Catholics, devotion to the Virgin Mary must be rooted in scripture.

Visitation miraculously pregnant cousins Mary and Elizabeth meet and rejoice (Luke 1:39–45).

wedding at Cana setting of Jesus's first miracle, changing water into wine (John 2:1–11).

References

Chapter 1: Meeting Mary: the surprising virgin

Pew Forum religious population figures, <http://www.pewforum.org/2012/12/18/global-religious-landscape-exec/>.

The Letters of St. Catherine of Siena, vol. 1, trans. Suzanne Noffke, OP (Medieval and Renaissance Texts and Studies, 1988) 38.

UNICEF statement against child marriage: <http://data.unicef.org/topic/child-protection/child-marriage/>.

Chapter 2: Mary in the New Testament, history, and earliest Christianity

New Testament assumes Jesus's normal birth proposed in Andrew T. Lincoln, *Born of a Virgin? Reconceiving Jesus in the Bible, Tradition, and Theology* (Eerdmans, 2013).

Ecumenical report on Virgin Mary in scripture: Raymond E. Brown, Paul J. Achtemeier, et al., *Mary in the New Testament: A Collaborative Assessment by Protestant and Roman Catholic Scholars* (Fortress Press, 1978) 206.

Mary's appearance: Luigi Gambero, 'Biographies of Mary in Byzantine Literature', *Marian Studies* 60 (2009) 43: <https://ecommons.udayton.edu/marian_studies/vol60/iss1/6>.

Chapter 3: Mary after the Gospels: new stories and evolving doctrine

'Mighty power in the heavens' (Pseudo-Cyril of Jerusalem): M. R. James, *Apocryphal New Testament* (1924) 8.

<https://archive.org/details/JAMESApocryphalNewTestament 1924/page/n37/mode/2up>.

Athanasius' warning: *Pachomian Koinonia I: The Lives, Rules and other Writings of Saint Pachomius and His Disciples*, trans. Armand Veilleux (Cistercian Publications, 1980) 230.

Mary feared death: cited in Stephen Shoemaker, 'The Ancient Dormition Apocrypha and the Origins of Marian Piety: Early Evidence of Marian Intercession from Late Ancient Palestine', in Leena M. Peltomaa, A. Külzer, and P. Allen, eds, *Presbeia Theothokou: The Intercessory Role of Mary across Times and Places in Byzantium (4th–9th Century)* (Austrian Academy of Sciences, 2015) 29.

Mary was baptized at Annunciation: Edmund Beck, OSB, 'Die Mariologie der echten Schriften Ephräms', *Oriens Christianus* 46 (1956) 28–9.

Re-dating Rylands Papyrus, *Sub tuum praesidium*: Theodore de Bruyn, 'Appeals to the Intercessions of Mary in Greek Liturgical and Paraliturgical Texts from Egypt', in Leena M. Peltomaa, A. Külzer, and P. Allen, eds, *Presbeia Theothokou* (Austrian Academy of Sciences Press, 2015) 114.

Joannia Amulet: AnneMarie Luijendijk, 'A Gospel Amulet for Joannia', in Kimberly B. Stratton and Dayna S. Kalleres, eds, *Daughters of Hecate: Women and Magic in the Ancient World* (Oxford, 2014) 418–43.

Epiphanius on the end of Mary's life: *Panarion* 78.23.9; Epiphanius of Salamis, *Panarion, Books II and III*, trans. Frank Williams (Brill, 1994) vol. 2, 619.

Dormition accounts, Marian intercession: Stephen Shoemaker, *Mary in Early Christian Faith and Devotion* (Yale, 2016) chapters 3 and 4 and 126–7.

Priestly Mary; Mary at the Last Supper: Ally Kateusz, *Mary and Early Christian Women: Hidden Leadership* (Palgrave Macmillan, 2019) 67–94; Christos Simelidis, 'Two Lives of the Virgin: John Geometres, Euthymios the Athonite, and Maximos the Confessor', *Dumbarton Oaks Papers* 74 (2020) 125–59.

Athanasius, *First Letter to Virgins* in David Brakke, *Athanasius and the Politics of Asceticism* (Oxford, 1995) 277–8.

Chapter 4: Mary the goddess?

No universal mother goddess: L. Goodison and C. Morris, 'Exploring Female Divinity: From Modern Myths to Ancient Evidence', in

L. Goodison and C. Morris, eds, *Ancient Goddesses* (British Museum Press, 1998) 6–21.

Carl Jung, *Answer to Job, Collected Works*, vol. 11 (Princeton, 1970) 72.

'Guest house of the Son of God', Richard of Saint-Laurent, *De laudibus beatae Mariae virginis*, cited in Rachel Fulton Brown, *Mary and the Art of Prayer* (Columbia University, 2018) 257.

Lawrence of Brindisi in Vernon Wagner, OFM Cap., trans., Sermon Five, 'The Singular Privileges of the Virgin Mother of God', from the *Mariale* by St Lawrence of Brindisi, *Round Table of Franciscan Research* 17 (1952) 32ff.

Shrine Madonna: Elina Gertsman, *Worlds Within: Opening the Medieval Shrine Madonna* (Penn State University Press, 2015). Image of German Shrine Madonna, *c.*1300, Metropolitan Museum of Art: <https://www.metmuseum.org/art/collection/search/464142>.

'Jesus Horus son of Isis': cited in David Frankfurter, *Christianizing Egypt: Syncretism and Local Worlds in Late Antiquity* (Princeton University Press, 2018) 1.

Magic spell, Mary Dissolving Chains: Marvin Meyer, 'The Persistence of Ritual in the Magical Book of Mary and the Angels: *P. Heid. Inv. Kopt. 685*', in April DeConick et al., eds, *Practicing Gnosis* (Brill, 2013) 371.

Augustine on God as mother: *Enarratio in Psalmum* 26, PL 36 cols 208–9.

Israelite goddess: William G. Dever, *Did God Have a Wife? Archaeology and Folk Religion in Ancient Israel* (Eerdmans, 2005).

Virgin of Montserrat, paint analysis: Elisa A. Foster, 'The Black Madonna of Montserrat: An Exception to the Concepts of Dark Skin in Medieval and Early Modern Iberia?', in Pamela A. Patton, ed., *Envisioning Others: Race, Color, and the Visual in Iberia and Latin America* (Brill, 2016) 26.

E. Ann Matter, 'The Virgin Mary: A Goddess?', in Carl Olsen, ed., *The Book of the Goddess* (Crossroads, 1983) 94.

Chapter 5: Eastern Mary—Byzantium and Islam

Proclus Homily I: N. Constas, *Proclus of Constantinople and the Cult of the Virgin in Late Antiquity: Homilies 1–5, Texts and Translations* (Brill, 2003) 128–47.

Pseudo-Athanasius on Jesus's conception: Constas, *Proclus of Constantinople*, 281.

Theodore Synkellos on Mary's mantle: Averil Cameron, 'The Virgin's Robe: An Episode in the History of Early Seventh-Century Constantinople', *Byzantion* 49 (1979) 53–4.

Confusion over Mary's relics; Bishop Juvenal relic legend: Annemarie Weyl Carr, 'Threads of Authority: The Virgin Mary's Veil in the Middle Ages', in Stewart Gordon, ed., *Robes of Honor: The Medieval World of Investiture* (Palgrave, 2001) 63; quotation: fn. 22.

Hymn about the mantle of the *Theotokos*: C. Mango, 'Constantinople as *Theotokopoulos*', in Maria Vassilaki, ed., *Mother of God* (Skira, 2000) 23.

Pussy Riot: Nicholas Denysenko, 'An Appeal to Mary: An Analysis of Pussy Riot's Punk Performance in Moscow', *Journal of the American Academy of Religion* 81 (2013) 1061–92.

Michael Psellos, quoted in B. Pentcheva, *Icons and Power: The Mother of God in Byzantium* (Penn State University, 2006) 154–61.

Mary approves Luke's portrait of her: Robin Cormack, *Writing in Gold: Byzantine Society and its Icons* (Oxford University Press, 1985) 126.

Zeitoun Apparitions: Sandrine Keriakos, 'Apparitions of the Virgin in Egypt: Improving Relations between Copts and Muslims?', in Dionigi Albera and Maria Couroucli, eds, *Sharing Sacred Spaces in the Mediterranean: Christians, Muslims, and Jews at Shrines and Sanctuaries* (Indiana University Press, 2012) 174–201.

Dome of the Rock Inscriptions: <https://www.islamic-awareness.org/history/islam/inscriptions/dotr>.

Qur'an quotations: *The Koran Interpreted*, trans. Arthur J. Arberry (Allen & Unwin; Macmillan, [1955]): <https://archive.org/details/QuranAJArberry/page/n1/mode/2up>.

Jesus's cradle: Nabil Matar, 'The Cradle of Jesus and the Oratory of Mary in Jerusalem's *al-Haram al-Sharif* ', *Jerusalem Quarterly* 70 (Summer, 2017) 112.

Ephraim of Syria, 'Nativity Hymn 6': Kathleen E. McVey, trans. & introd., *Ephrem the Syrian Hymns* (Paulist, 1989) 111; (as 'Nativity Hymn 4': <https://www.newadvent.org/fathers/3703.htm>).

Muslim women at Mary shrines: Willy Jansen and Meike Kühl, 'Shared Symbols: Muslims, Marian Pilgrimages and Gender', *European Journal of Women's Studies* 15.3 (2008) 295–311.

Mary image in *Ka'ba*: Alfred Guillaume, *The Life of Muhammad: A translation of Ishaq's 'Sirat Rasul Allah'* (Oxford University Press, 1955) 552.

Iranian film, *Saint Mary* (2000) dir. Shahriar Bahrani (English dubbing): <https://www.youtube.com/watch?v=oWjz1z4oEls>.

Muhammad claimed (hadith) Mary and Jesus were preserved from Satan: Al-Tabari, *Tafsīr*, VII, 96–7.

Mary hopes her newborn will defend her, in Syriac hymn: Sebastian Brock, 'A Dialog between Joseph and Mary', *Welsh Theological Review* 1.3 (1992) 4–11.

Chapter 6: Empress of heaven and hell: Mary in the Middle Ages and Renaissance

Henry Adams, *Education of Henry Adams* (Houghton Mifflin, 1918) chapter 25, 'The Dynamo and the Virgin (1900)'.

Bonaventure on Mary Queen of Mercy: Hilde Graef and Thomas A. Thomson, *Mary: A History of Doctrine and Devotion*, rev. edn (Ave Maria, 2009) 227.

Bernardino of Siena on the Virgin's power: Donna Spivey Ellington, *From Sacred Body to Angelic Soul: Understanding Mary in Late Medieval and Early Modern Europe* (Catholic University of America, 2001) 60.

Fulbert of Chartres on Jesus's respect for his mother: Margot Fassler, 'Mary's Nativity, Fulbert of Chartres, and the *Stirps Jesse*: Liturgical Innovation circa 1000 and Its Afterlife', *Speculum* 75.2 (2000) 406.

Meditations on the Life of Christ by John of Caulibus, trans. Francis X. Taney, Anne Miller, and C. Mary Stallings-Taney (Pegasus, 2000) 13, 28.

Meditation on Mary's beauty and body, cited in Kathryn M. Rudy, *Rubrics, Images and Indulgences in Late Medieval Netherlandish Manuscripts* (Brill, 2017) 173.

Medieval gynaecology: Charles T. Wood, 'The Doctor's Dilemma: Sin, Salvation, and the Menstrual Cycle in Medieval Thought', *Speculum* 56.4 (1981) 710–27.

Rupert of Deutz cited in Rachel Fulton, *From Judgment to Passion: Devotion to Christ and the Virgin Mary, 800–1200* (Columbia University Press, 2002) 324.

Joseph's Doubt (medieval Mystery Play): <https://d.lib.rochester.edu/teams/text/sugano-n-town-plays-play-12-josephs-doubt>.

Philip of Harvengt, Mary as Bride of Christ: Hilde Graef and Thomas A. Thomson, *Mary: A History of Doctrine and Devotion*, rev. edn (Ave Maria, 2009) 200.

Bernardino of Siena on Mary conceiving Jesus: Hilde Graef and
Thomas A. Thomson, *Mary: A History of Doctrine and Devotion*,
rev. edn (Ave Maria, 2009) 249.

Anti-Jewish images in Books of Hours: Denise L. Despres,
'Immaculate Flesh and the Social Body: Mary and the Jews', *Jewish
History* 12.1 (1998) 49.

Sacred romances: Maureen Barry McCann Boulton, *Sacred Fictions of
Medieval France: Narrative Theology in the Lives of Christ and the
Virgin 1150–1500* (Boydell and Brewer, 2015) 36–8.

Virgin statues outnumber crucifixes: Amy Remensnyder, 'The
Colonization of Sacred Architecture: The Virgin Mary, Mosques,
and Temples in Medieval Spain and Early Sixteenth-Century
Mexico', in Sharon Farmer and Barbara H. Rosenwein, eds, *Monks
and Nuns, Saints and Outcasts: Religion in Medieval Society*
(Cornell University Press, 2000) 201.

Chapter 7: Modern Mary—Reformation to the present

Marian images in Protestant Germany: Bridget Heal, *The Cult of the
Virgin Mary in Early Modern Germany: Protestant and Catholic
Piety, 1500–1648* (Cambridge University Press, 2007) 23, 76.

Marriage as sacrament: Philip L. Reynolds, *How Marriage Became
One of the Sacraments: The Sacramental Theology of Marriage
from Its Medieval Origins to the Council of Trent* (Cambridge
University Press, 2016), chapter 1.

Mary as Buddhist *Kannon*: Junhyoung Michael Shin, 'Avalokiteśvara's
Manifestation as the Virgin Mary: The Jesuit Adaptation and the
Visual Conflation in Japanese Catholicism after 1614', *Church
History* 80.1 (2011) 11–12.

Nahua people believed God's name was Mary: Amy Remensnyder,
'The Colonization of Sacred Architecture: The Virgin Mary,
Mosques, and Temples in Medieval Spain and Early Sixteenth-
Century Mexico', in Sharon Farmer and Barbara H. Rosenwein,
eds, *Monks and Nuns, Saints and Outcasts: Religion in Medieval
Society* (Cornell University Press, 2000) fn. 90, p. 208.

'Vernacular religion': Nathan D. Mitchell, *The Mystery of the Rosary:
Marian Devotion and the Reinvention of Catholicism* (New York
University Press, 2009) 122.

Further reading

Chapter 1: Meeting Mary: the surprising virgin

Sarah Jane Boss, ed., *Mary: The Complete Resource* (Oxford University Press, 2007).

Hilde Graef and Thomas A. Thomson, *Mary: A History of Doctrine and Devotion*, rev. edn (Ave Maria, 2009).

Amy-Jill Levine, ed., *A Feminist Companion to Mariology* (T and T Clark, 2005).

Chris Maunder, ed., *Oxford Handbook of the Virgin Mary* (Oxford University Press, 2019).

Miri Rubin, *Mother of God: A History of the Virgin Mary* (Penguin, 2009).

Timothy Verdon, Melissa R. Katz, Amy G. Remensnyder, and Miri Rubin, eds, *Picturing Mary: Woman, Mother, Idea*; Exhibition Catalogue, National Museum of Women in the Arts, Washington, DC, 5 Dec 2014–12 Apr 2015 (Scala Arts, 2014).

Marina Warner, *Alone of All Her Sex: The Myth and the Cult of the Virgin Mary* (Vintage, 1983; orig. pub. 1976).

Chapter 2: Mary in the New Testament, history, and earliest Christianity

Raymond E. Brown, Paul J. Achtemeier, et al., *Mary in the New Testament: A Collaborative Assessment by Protestant and Roman Catholic Scholars* (Fortress, 1978).

Mary F. Foskett, *A Virgin Conceived: Mary and Classical Representations of Virginity* (Indiana University, 2002).

Ronald F. Hock, 'The Favored One: How Mary Became the Mother of God', *Bible Review* 17.3 (June 2001).

Mary Joan Winn Leith, 'Mary, the Mother of Jesus', *Oxford Encyclopedia of the Books of the Bible* (Oxford University Press, published online 2011).

Chapter 3: Mary after the Gospels: new stories and evolving doctrine

Sebastian Brock, *Bride of Light: Hymns on Mary from the Syriac Churches* (Gorgias, 2010).

Apocryphal texts: J. K. Elliott, *Apocryphal New Testament: A Collection of Apocryphal Christian Literature in an English Translation* (Oxford University Press, 1993); <http://gnosis.org/library/cac.htm>.

Luigi Gambero, *Mary and the Fathers of the Church: The Blessed Virgin Mary in Patristic Thought*, trans. Thomas Buffer (Ignatius, 1999).

Ally Kateusz, *Mary and Early Christian Women: Hidden Leadership* (Palgrave Macmillan, 2019).

Mary Joan Winn Leith, 'Earliest Depictions of the Virgin Mary', *Biblical Archaeology Review* 43.2 (2017) 40–9, 68–70.

Brian K. Reynolds, *Gateway to Heaven: Marian Doctrine and Devotion, Image and Typology in the Patristic and Medieval Periods*, vol. 1 (New City, 2012).

Stephen Shoemaker, *Mary in Early Christian Faith and Devotion* (Yale University Press, 2016).

Chapter 4: Mary the goddess?

Stephen Benko, *The Virgin Goddess: Studies in the Pagan and Christian Roots of Mariology* (Brill, 1993).

Lucy Goodison and Christine Morris, eds, *Ancient Goddesses: The Myths and the Evidence* (British Museum, 1998).

E. Ann Matter, 'The Virgin Mary: A Goddess?', in Carl Olsen, ed., *The Book of the Goddess* (Crossroads, 1983) 80–96.

Monique Scheer, 'From Majesty to Mystery: Change in the Meanings of Black Madonnas from the Sixteenth to Nineteenth Centuries', *American Historical Review* 107.5 (2002) 1412–40.

Chapter 5: Eastern Mary—Byzantium and Islam

Byzantine/Orthodox:

Leslie Brubaker and Mary B. Cunningham, eds, *The Cult of the Mother of God in Byzantium* (Ashgate, 2011).

Mary Cunningham, *The Gateway of Life: Orthodox Thinking on the Mother of God* (SVS, 2015).

Bissera Pentcheva, *Icons and Power: The Mother of God in Byzantium* (Pennsylvania State University, 2008).

Maria Vassilaki, ed., *Images of the Mother of God: Perceptions of the Theotokos in Byzantium* (Ashgate, 2005).

Islam:

Jonathan M. Reck, 'The Annunciation to Mary: A Christian Echo in the Qur'an', *Vigiliae Christianae* 68 (2014) 355–83.

Barbara Stowasser, 'Mary in the Qur'an', chapter 7, *Women in the Qur'an: Traditions and Interpretations* (Oxford University Press, 1994) 67–82.

Chapter 6: Empress of heaven and hell: Mary in the Middle Ages and Renaissance

Sarah Jane Boss, *Empress and Handmaid: On Nature and Gender in the Cult of the Virgin Mary* (Cassell, 2000).

John of Caulibus (Pseudo-Bonaventure), *Meditations on the Life of Christ*, trans. Francis X Taney, Anne Miller, and C. Mary Stallings-Taney (Pegasus, 2000).

Rachel Fulton, *From Judgment to Passion: Devotion to Christ and the Virgin Mary, 800–1200* (Columbia University Press, 2002).

R. N. Swanson, ed., *The Church and Mary* (Boydell, 2004).

Jacobus de Voragine, *The Golden Legend*, 2 vols.; trans. William Granger Ryan (Princeton University Press, 1993).

Chapter 7: Modern Mary—Reformation to the present

Virgil Elizondo, *Guadalupe: Mother of the New Creation* (Orbis, 1997).

Ruth Harris, *Lourdes: Body and Spirit in the Secular Age* (Penguin, 1999).

Elizabeth A. Johnson, *Truly our Sister: A Theology of Mary in the Communion of Saints* (Continuum, 2003).

Nathan D. Mitchell, *The Mystery of the Rosary: Marian Devotion and the Reinvention of Catholicism* (New York University Press, 2009).

Robert Anthony Orsi, *The Madonna of 115th Street: Faith and Community in Italian Harlem, 1880–1950* (Yale University Press, 1985).

'Our Lady', chapter VIII in the *Dogmatic Constitution on the Church—Lumen Gentium*, Promulgated By His Holiness, Pope Paul VI, 21 November 1964. <https://www.vatican.va/archive/hist_councils/ii_vatican_council/documents/vat-ii_const_19641121_lumen-gentium_en.html>.

Amy G. Remensnyder, *La Conquistadora: The Virgin Mary at War and Peace in the Old and New Worlds* (Oxford University Press, 2014).

Monique Scheer, 'Catholic Piety in the Early Cold War Years or How the Virgin Mary Protected the West from Communism', in Annette Vowinckel, Marcus M. Payk, and Thomas Lindenberger, eds, *Cold War Cultures: Perspectives on Eastern and Western European Societies* (Berghan Books, 2012) 129–51.

Elizabeth Schussler-Fiorenza, 'Mariology, Gender Ideology and the Discipleship of Equals', in Elizabeth Schussler-Fiorenza, *Transforming Vision: Explorations in Feminist The*logy* (Fortress, 2011) 197–213.

Sandra L. Zimdars-Swartz, *Encountering Mary: From La Salette to Medjugorje* (Princeton University Press, 1991).

Index

For the benefit of digital users, indexed terms that span two pages (e.g., 52–53) may, on occasion, appear on only one of those pages.

CATHOLICISM
A Very Short Introduction
Gerald O'Collins

Despite a long history of external threats and internal strife, the
Roman Catholic Church and the broader reality of Catholicism
remain a vast and valuable presence into the third millennium of
world history. What are the origins of the Catholic Church? How
has Catholicism changed and adapted to such vast and diverse
cultural influences over the centuries? What great challenges
does the Catholic Church now face in the twenty-first century,
both within its own life and in its relation to others around the
world? In this Very Short Introduction, Gerald O'Collins draws on
the best current scholarship available to answer these questions
and to present, in clear and accessible language, a fresh
introduction to the largest and oldest institution in the world.

www.oup.com/vsi

CHRISTIAN ETHICS
A Very Short Introduction
D. Stephen Long

This *Very Short Introduction* to Christian ethics introduces the topic by examining its sources and historical basis. D. Stephen Long presents a discussion of the relationship between Christian ethics, modern, and postmodern ethics, and explores practical issues including sex, money, and power. Long recognises the inherent difficulties in bringing together 'Christian' and 'ethics' but argues that this is an important task for both the Christian faith and for ethics. Arguing that Christian ethics are not a precise science, but the cultivation of practical wisdom from a range of sources, Long also discusses some of the failures of the Christian tradition, including the crusades, the conquest, slavery, inquisitions, and the Galileo affair.

www.oup.com/vsi

THOMAS AQUINAS
A Very Short Introduction
Fergus Kerr

Thomas Aquinas, an Italian Catholic priest in the early thirteenth century, is considered to be one of the great Christian thinkers who had, and who still has, a profound influence on Western thought. He was a controversial figure who was exposed and engaged in conflict. This *Very Short Introduction* looks at Aquinas in a historical context, and explores the Church and culture into which Aquinas was born. It considers Aquinas as philosopher, and looks at the relationship between philosophy and religion in the thirteenth century. Fergus Kerr, in this engaging and informative introduction, will make *The Summa Theologiae*, Aquinas's greatest single work, accessible to new readers. It will also reflect on the importance of Thomas Aquinas in modern debates and asks why Aquinas matters now.

www.oup.com/vsi

THE NEW TESTAMENT
A Very Short Introduction
Luke Timothy Johnson

As part of the Christian Bible, the New Testament is at once widely influential and increasingly unknown. Those who want to know the basics can find in this introduction the sort of information that locates these ancient writings in their historical and literary context. In addition to providing the broad conceptual and factual framework for the New Testament — including the process by which distinct compositions became a sacred book — this introduction provides as well a more detailed examination of specific compositions that have had particularly strong influence, including Paul's letters to the Corinthians and Romans, the four Gospels, and the Book of Revelation.

www.oup.com/vsi

SCIENCE AND RELIGION
A Very Short Introduction
Thomas Dixon

The debate between science and religion is never out of the news: emotions run high, fuelled by polemical bestsellers and, at the other end of the spectrum, high-profile campaigns to teach 'Intelligent Design' in schools. Yet there is much more to the debate than the clash of these extremes. As Thomas Dixon shows in this balanced and thought-provoking introduction, many have seen harmony rather than conflict between faith and science. He explores not only the key philosophical questions that underlie the debate, but also the social, political, and ethical contexts that have made 'science and religion' such a fraught and interesting topic in the modern world, offering perspectives from non-Christian religions and examples from across the physical, biological, and social sciences.

'A rich introductory text . . . on the study of relations of science and religion.'

R. P. Whaite, Metascience

www.oup.com/vsi

PENTECOSTALISM
A Very Short Introduction
William K. Kay

In religious terms Pentecostalism was probably the most
vibrant and rapidly-growing religious movement of the 20th
century. Starting as a revivalistic and renewal movement within
Christianity, it encircled the globe in less than 25 years and
grew in North America and then in those parts of the world
with the highest birth-rates. Characterised by speaking in
tongues, miracles, television evangelism and megachurches, it
is also noted for its small-group meetings, empowerment of
individuals, liberation of women and humanitarian concerns.
William K Kay outlines the origins and growth of
Pentecostalism, looking at not only the theological aspects of
the movement, but also the sociological influences of its
political and humanitarian viewpoints.

www.oup.com/vsi